Rally Manual

edited by Peter Browning

PSL

Patrick Stephens, London

First published - September 1971.
Reprinted - January 1972.

ISBN 0 85059 076 0.

Text set in 9 on 10 pt Times Roman. Printed in Great Britain on Trueblade 118gm² for Patrick Stephens Limited, 9 Ely Place, London EC1N 6SQ, by Blackfriars Press Limited, Leicester LE5 4BS. Bound by Hunter & Foulis Limited, Edinburgh EH7 4NP.

Contents

Editor's introduction

INTERNATIONAL RALLYING has not in the past been particularly well documented, and it is intended that this publication will fill two significant needs.

In the first half of the book I have invited acknowledged rallying experts to write about the subject that most interests them at the present time. I hope that these features will educate the novice, appeal to the amateur clubman and even entertain the professional.

There has, up till now, been no standard reference book on rallying and I also hope that the second half of this manual will serve that purpose. I know that it will be well thumbed by those whose business involves them in the sport of rallying. It should also be of use to those who are interested in facts and figures and who want to know more about rally cars and drivers.

This book is the first of its kind and, as such, is a gamble both for its sponsors and publishers. I must therefore thank Castrol for backing the idea and the publishers, Patrick Stephens Ltd, for having faith in my claim that it will find its way into the pocket of every enthusiast's rally jacket!

PETER BROWNING
Hendon, London

September 1971

The Editor would like to record his grateful thanks to the following companies and individuals for their help in providing photographs with which to illustrate this book: Alpine-Renault, Autocar, Hugh Bishop, British Leyland, Burmah-Castrol, Michael Cooper, Esler Crawford, Chrysler UK, John Davenport, Ford, Motor, Motoring News, Opel, Geraint Phillips, Saab, Colin Taylor Productions. Front cover picture: Roger Clark/Jim Porter (Ford Escort Twin Cam) 1970 Scottish Rally. Inside front cover: Timo Makinen/Tony Fall (Mini-Cooper 'S') on the televised stage held in place of the cancelled 1967 RAC Rally. Inside back cover: Tom Trana/Solve Andreasson (Saab V4). Back cover: Brian Culcheth/Johnstone Syer (Triumph 2.5) 1970 Scottish Rally.

CHAPTER 1

So you want to be a rally driver

Brian Culcheth, former British Leyland works driver and the highest-placed British driver on the World Cup Rally, explains the art of rough road driving

---

TRYING TO TEACH other people to acquire the art of rally driving is a lot more difficult than trying to do it yourself, and it is a subject that is better taught from the driving seat than the armchair. Without knowing the proficiency of my readers I have supposed in the following explanations that they have not got much further than thinking rather more seriously about their driving than the average motorist, and that they wish to learn more about advanced techniques. The following, therefore, may seem elementary to the more experienced competition drivers but I hope that they, too, may find something to interest and educate them.

I have put the emphasis on the technique of rough road driving because this will be the aspect of rally driving that is of most interest. Forestry rallying is the backbone of British club events and becomes the first step up the ladder for the ambitious clubman after the lesser navigational rallies.

Are you sitting comfortably?

Let's begin with the driving position, for you cannot hope to drive properly (even on normal long-distance road motoring) if you are not seated correctly and are not able to operate the controls with ease.

Because the pedals of very few cars are adjustable you should first set the seat to a position that best suits the pedals. Having got that right, you can then 'tune' your driving position in relation to the steering wheel, either by adjusting the steering column (if adjustment is provided) or by fitting a different steering wheel, dished or flat according to your choice. The seat should be in a position where you can depress the pedals to their extremes without quite having your leg at full stretch, for this can become very tiring on a long journey.

Most top-line rally men prefer to sit rather closer to the wheel than is possible when adopting the current straight-arm driving position favoured by racing drivers. Even on short rallies your arms will get very tired held out in the fully extended position and, for rough road driving, you will not be in the best position to get a really strong grip of the wheel. The arms should be in a relaxed and slightly bent position, to naturally hold the wheel at around the 'quarter to three' position. You should also be able to take a firm hold of the wheel at the '12 o'clock' position without stretching.

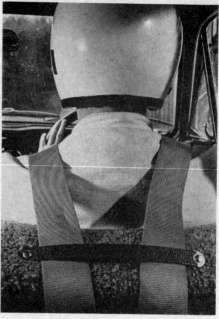

Above left: Features of the ideal driving position—leather rim wheel with spoke coverings, driving gloves, comfortable overalls, easy location of the handbrake, wide lap strap belt, overdrive switch on the gear lever, controls grouped for easy operation.

Above right: Strap to hold the twin shoulder belts in position.

Left: Accelerator pedal modified for easy heel and toe operation.

CASTROL RALLY MANUAL

The height of the seat should be considered next, and most rally drivers tend to sit rather higher than the standard position so that they can get a better view of the road immediately ahead. This is more important on a car with a long bonnet, like the Triumph 2.5PI, than the snub-nosed Mini-Cooper. The seat must provide firm but not hard support and, above all, there must be good lateral location. The leading edges of the seat cushion should be well-rounded to avoid restricting the blood circulation in the legs.

I have never favoured a reclining seat for the driver because these usually have a small gap at the joint of the backrest and the cushion—the place where support is most needed. By the nature of their construction they also lose some strength with the adjustable back-rest. If you are entering events where the co-driver has to take the wheel the seat may need adequate fore-and-aft adjustment. If not, then the seat is best bolted straight to the floor. The seat covering should give good grip, and be warm in winter and cool in summer. The modern brushed nylon trim seems to be the best.

Belt up

A full safety harness is essential for rough road rallying and most drivers favour the type with individually adjustable shoulder straps, a single quick-release buckle for all four straps and a wide lap strap that gives comfortable support. As with all belts, it must be a design that is easily put on and instantly adjustable. It is useful to have the shoulder straps held together with a piece of elastic just behind the seat so that they do not fall down behind when you take them off and, when you are relaxing on a road section, you can release the tension a little without them falling off your shoulders.

The pedals should be adjusted or modified so that it is possible to operate the throttle and the brake by swivelling the foot on the heel rather than having to lift it off one pedal and on to the other. This may involve alterations to both the pedals' travel and positions but it is worthwhile because it can become very tiring to have to lift your foot off the floor with every application of the brake.

The pedals should also be adjusted to a position where it is possible to 'heel and toe', a technique which permits you to operate the brake with the toe and the throttle with the heel at the same time. According to the layout of the pedals this can either be achieved by angling the foot across both pedals (with the toe on the brake and the heel on the throttle) or, if the pedals are close enough, by putting the foot across the two pedals and operating both at the same time by rocking the foot.

The purpose of the heel and toe operation is to enable you to make the appropriate gear change while at the same time applying continuous braking. If you are not able to heel and toe then you must either make the gear change without adjusting the engine revs (which will be hard on the synchromesh and the clutch) or you will have to make repeated time-wasting applications of the brake as you alternate between brake and throttle.

Controls

Most rally drivers prefer a steering wheel with a thickly padded leather rim which enables you to get a firm grip on rough roads, and the soft padding helps to dampen out some of the shocks. It is important that the leather covering should continue for a little way along the spokes so that this gives protection for the thumbs. It is amazing that many high-performance cars, which are renowned for their safety, are fitted with wood-rimmed wheels that are lethal in the event of a serious accident for the rim can splinter and inflict terrible injuries.

The gear lever position should be considered next and the driver should be able to reach the conventional 'first' and 'third' positions without stretching. The gear lever knob, un-like those on many production cars, should be smooth and round without any sharp edges or knurled surfaces which can cause a nasty sore on long-distance events. If the car is fitted with an overdrive, then the switch should be mounted on the gear lever.

The handbrake should be of the fly-off type and come readily to hand. It should be fitted with a solid hand grip if one is not provided by the manufacturer.

All controls should be within comfortable reach and grouped in a logical position, which is often not the case with production cars. The fog lamp switches should be paired away from the driving lamp switches, as should the controls for the windscreen wiper and washer. All should be set up for single-handed operation.

As far as instruments are concerned, the rev counter should have the prominent position and be so angled that the needle comes up to the vertical position when the engine is at maximum revs. The oil pressure and water temperature gauges are the next most important; the fuel gauge is best placed in a position where it can be seen by both members of the crew and things like the alternator or dynamo charge are best indicated by warning lights rather than gauges.

Personal

While a lot of people go rallying, even on international events, in casual clothing, at the risk of being called a boy racer I prefer to wear flameproof overalls at all times. This not only makes good sense as far as safety is concerned, but I find that they are extremely comfortable, give good breathing and are warm in winter and cool in summer. They are designed for the job, with pockets in the right places and close-fitting cuffs and trouser bottoms. With improved heating systems and fresh-air ventilation for both members of the crew, there is no need to go rallying dressed like an Eskimo. Inevitably, on any event you are going to have to 'get out and get under' and you're going to get dirty. I have found that it is a lot cheaper to get a pair of overalls dirty and perhaps torn than to ruin everyday clothing.

Most drivers wear gloves because sweaty hands are both unpleasant and dangerous. I favour the fully backed glove rather than the open-backed type because these can, in hectic moments, get caught up in window winders, etc, and I prefer a lightweight leather driving shoe with a built-up heel. Leather soles dry off quicker than rubber and give a better grip on the pedals. Obviously your crash helmet must be comfortable and there must be no pressure on any part of the head. A helmet which feels comfortable on a four-minute forestry stage on the RAC Rally may give you a cracking headache after three hours on the London-Sydney Marathon! An intercom set is well worth the money if you're going for the big-time events for it is a great advantage to be able to communicate with your co-driver at normal volume.

I have gone into the preceding items at some length because I consider that they contribute a great deal to one's ability to perform the more sophisticated techniques which are described later. More than one rally has been lost when a foot slipped off a badly positioned pedal or a driver in a tight position had to hang on to the wheel instead of being able to steer his way out of trouble. Undoubtedly many poor performances could have been attributed to the fact that the crew had not taken the trouble to pay attention to their comfort. If you have ambitions to be a professional rally driver then at least these are the things that anyone can get right.

Lighting

It is equally important that you have the car properly set up before the start of the event. How often have you seen drivers adjusting their lights half way through the first night?

Setting up the lights is vitally important for there is little point in having the fastest car in the event if you cannot see where you are going! Everyone has their own preference but

Ideal line for the hairpin bend, close to the apex and power-sliding the tail.

I prefer to have both the long beam lamps set for maximum long vision. The lights should be set up on a flat piece or road, preferably with some distinguishing feature at the point of maximum range. Twin fog lights should be angled outwards so that they pick out the verges and assist with acute cornering; this can be achieved in two ways. You can either have the lights fitted on the outside of the car facing outwards or they can be mounted towards the centre of the car and angled inwards with crossed beams. I prefer the latter set up because, with main beams adjusted for maximum length, the crossed fog beams tend to fill in the dark patch immediately in front of the car. Many drivers, particularly on hilly forestry rallies, prefer to have their long range lights set one up and one down. This gives less penetration on the level but you do have the advantage of being able to see up and down the hills.

It is equally important to spend some time testing and adjusting the screen washers. If you have a four-jet system, with a double jet for each side, it is worthwhile setting one jet up and one jet down to get maximum coverage of the screen. Test them fully at rally speeds before the event.

Steering

Now that you are properly clothed and comfortably seated in the car with all the final adjustments made, we can consider some of the more elementary techniques of driving.

With the direct action of current steering geometries and smaller steering wheels, most cars can be handled through most manoeuvres by holding the hands in the 'quarter to three' position and by crossing the arms in the manner not approved of by your driving instructor! You should always try and keep one hand on the wheel in a fixed position so

The Scandinavians make use of the scenery to achieve the ultimate performance but snow-banks are kinder on the bodywork than the traditional British forestry earth bank!

It is not always possible to land straight but it's a lot easier on the suspension if you can land 'all square'.

that when you come out of the corner (and particularly on ice and snow) you are always able to find the straight-ahead position.

With gearchanging, many drivers are reluctant to break their traditional sequence of using all the ratios. Time and wear on the transmission can be saved by changing straight from top to second or even from third to first gear. With overdrive this is where it is very important to have the switch on the gear lever knob. Novice drivers seldom use the gearbox enough and, if you listen to the works driver through a stage, you will hear that he constantly changes the ratios to keep the engine on maximum torque. This is not to say that you should be hard on the gearbox; the changes should be quick but not fast enough to beat the syncromesh.

Handbrake turns

It would be a lucky crew that did not wrong slot or overshoot a junction on a rally and have to retrace their steps, often turning round in a restricted space. It is here that the handbrake turn, the popular manoeuvre of the driving test exponent, can be very useful. It can also be used to advantage on very tight hairpin bends and acute road junctions when a shuffle turn with reversing would otherwise be necessary.

With a front-wheel drive car the handbrake turn is accomplished by turning the wheel into the corner, keeping the foot hovering on the throttle and, at the same moment, pulling up the handbrake to lock the rear wheels. This will bring the tail of the car round in a slide and when the car is facing in the right direction it can be driven out of the turn by releasing the handbrake and accelerating away.

With rear-wheel drive the procedure is the same except that the car should be steered into the corner before applying the handbrake and the clutch should be depressed through the turn. The car can be brought out of the turn by releasing the handbrake, easing in the clutch and converting the slide into forward movement.

Although it is possible to perform 180 degree and even 360 degree turns on dry tarmac, this needs considerable skill and courage. It is very easy, even with a modest experiment, to put the car on its side, especially if you are using normal high-grip road or racing tyres. The novice is strongly advised to practice on a loose, slippery surface well away from obstacles!

Hairpins

Let us next consider the hairpin bend. The secret here is to be as neat and tidy as possible, for often the conventional racing driver's style is faster than the sideways technique of the rally man. If you go into the corner too fast then, with rear-wheel drive, you will probably understeer away from the apex and lose time as you have insufficient momentum to power the tail round to complete the turn. Too fast with front-wheel drive will probably force you to do a dramatic handbrake turn, which could well bring you to an ignominious standstill on the apex of the bend, from where you will have to make a time-wasting restart.

The correct approach should be to take the racing driver's line, cutting the apex of the corner as tight as possible and powering the tail round. Generally the old motto, 'slow in fast out' serves best. The same principles apply to both uphill and downhill hairpins.

Cornering technique

For high-speed cornering on a dirt road the same basic principles apply to both front- and rear-wheel drive cars. The subject is best explained by reference to the accompanying diagrams, which show a straightforward right-angle corner (figure 1) and a rather more acute right-hand turn (figure 2). We should assume in both examples that the turn is preceded by a long high-speed straight.

Our object is to get from point A on the diagrams to point D as quickly and as safely as possible. In normal conventional fast driving at point A, or even before, you would have started to slow for the corner, probably by braking and changing from top to third gear. The normal cornering technique would involve more severe braking between points A and B, with perhaps a heel and toe change from third to second gear. Soon after point B the car would be turned into the corner to cut the apex at point C. Firm acceleration would be applied throughout the turn, with full power being applied soon after point C as the car accelerates towards our imaginary finishing line, point D.

The rally driver's technique would be a lot different, considerably faster and, assuming that you were driving the corner blind without previous knowledge, it would also be a lot safer. The first and the most significant advantage that the rally driver would have would be between points A and B. Here he would continue well beyond point A at maximum speed knowing that the techniques he was about to employ would provide both adequate stopping and cornering power.

This technique is based on the fact that a wheel that is moving sideways on a dirt road gives very much better retardation than a wheel that is being braked in a straight line. The main reason for this is that the dirt piles up against the sidewall of the tyre and provides a considerable braking effect. The longer the slide the greater retardation the dirt provides. Secondly, all four wheels will be going sideways, thus an equal braking effect is applied.

By unbalancing the car in position 1 in figure 1 considerable braking effect is applied, but you will notice that the car is first swung to the left, against the direction of the corner. This preparatory movement is achieved as follows. On smooth dirt roads in position 1 a quick half turn flick of the steering wheel is given to the left, followed immediately by an over-correcting steering movement to the right. On most loose surfaces this will be sufficient to put the car into position 3, but it may also be necessary to break the tail away by applying a stab of throttle. On rutted dirt roads, or on rutted ice, at position 1 the car is brought out of the ruts with the left wheels up on the loose verge and the right wheels riding up on the centre ridge. As soon as the rear wheels have climbed out of the ruts the front wheels are put back in the ruts and, with a rear-wheel drive car, a sharp stab of the throttle will have car set up in position 3, pointing towards the apex of the corner. With a front-wheel drive car the very action of putting the front wheels back into the ruts will probably be enough to unbalance the car into position 3.

All of these manoeuvres can be carried out under severe braking if necessary which, combined with the sideways attitude of the car, first in one direction and then the other, will have reduced the speed by the required amount. Certainly, it will have been more effective than the normal straight-line braking method.

With the car approaching point 4, now for the first time we are able to see the severity of the corner, but we are nevertheless in the only safe position to take the necessary action. If the corner continues, as in figure 1, then by throttle and steering control through positions 5, 6 and 7 we can change the attitude of the car into a straight-ahead position, driving out of the corner in the conventional manner. If, however, the corner has tightened, as in figure 2, then only from position 4 would we stand a chance of getting out of trouble.

With a rear-wheel drive car from position 4 in figure 2 you would apply more power and steer more into the corner to power the tail round the more acute angle. With front-wheel drive, by lifting the throttle at position 4 (and perhaps by left foot braking, which is described later) this would similarly pull the car round towards the apex.

Except in positions 1-4, when we have deliberately put the car sideways to achieve maximum braking, always remember that the object should be to get the car back into a

12

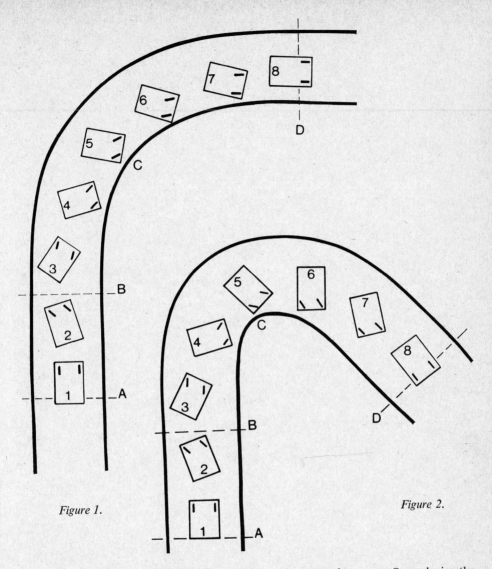

Figure 1.

Figure 2.

straight line as soon as possible, for this is the fastest means of progress. Over-playing the sideways attitude beyond position 6, hanging the tail out into the verge and spraying the spectators with gravel, may be good for your ego but it will not improve your stage times!

The merits of this technique are well illustrated if you consider how our conventional driver would have fared if, when driving the corner blind, he arrived at point C too fast or, worse still, then found that the corner was more acute, as in figure 2. By the time he realised the situation it would be impossible for him to get the car into a sideways attitude. In trying to achieve this he may spin somewhere around positions 6 or 7 in figure 1 or understeer off the road at a point well north of position 6. In the case of the more acute corner in figure 2 he would most certainly understeer straight off into the undergrowth!

Front- or rear-wheel drive?

The merits of front- or rear-wheel drive in such circumstances are hard to determine. If the severity of the corner is known then I would favour rear-wheel drive, particularly the tail-heavy slightly oversteering rear-engined rear-wheel drive cars like the Porsche 911 or the Alpine-Renault. A car so balanced is very much easier to control in manoeuvres like those in positions 1-3 and can more easily maintain the attitude of positions 4-7. If, however, the corner is not known, and it suddenly tightens as in figure 2, then rear-wheel drive is at a disadvantage because the powered end of the car is constantly moving dangerously towards the outside of the corner. This may be on to the loose verge which would provide less grip or, more serious, it may be over the edge of an Alpine drop!

With front-wheel drive, given adequate power and traction, one is always able to steer the driving wheels into the best position for grip, and it does not really matter what happens to the tail of the car. Front-wheel drive cars are a lot more forgiving in unexpected and dangerous circumstances, and certainly a lot faster downhill on loose surfaces. That advantage, however, is lost when going uphill when, given equal power and weight, rear-engined rear-wheel drive will always score.

Sideways for safety

Many novices are, quite naturally, not a little alarmed when the car goes sideways. After all, it is not a natural thing to do and, up till now, all of one's driving technique has probably been aimed at preventing such a thing from happening. It takes confidence, a good sense of feel and balance, but above all a lot of practice. Rallycross and autocross, and even autotests, are good practice in car control but, because there is usually plenty of space around, these are no substitutes for forestry rallying, where you have got to be a lot more precise.

Left foot braking

The art of left foot braking was first used by the Scandinavians in ice and snow driving and is the basis of their high-speed rally driving technique. It is, however, seldom practised by non-Scandinavians and Paddy Hopkirk and Roger Clark have proved that they can get along quite well without resort to such manoeuvres. Most of us feel that we do not get enough practice in loose road driving to learn to do it naturally and, if you cannot do it naturally, then you are better not to do it at all! It has its best advantage on front-wheel drive cars, but it can also be used on rear-wheel drive.

The theory is similar to that already described for the handbrake turn but, instead of using the handbrake to lock the rear wheels, the left foot is stamped on the brake which, with front-wheel drive, will have much the same effect. The rear wheels of the car will be momentarily locked, thus turning the car into the corner. The front wheels, because the driving force of the engine under power will over-ride the brakes, continue to power the car in the normal manner.

With our previous example, left foot braking could be used to advantage in position 4 in figure 2. With power being applied to the front wheels and more right lock, the left foot would be stamped upon the brakes, once and very hard, which would turn the car into the corner.

Because you are asking the car, or more correctly, the transmission, to do two opposing things at the same time, left foot braking if used extensively can be very hard on the car. Timo Makinen was the king of left foot braking with the Mini and he used it so much that when he came off a long special stage his rear brakes would often be so hot that they would literally catch fire!

Setting the car up in the opposite direction to the corner before the bend. In this case, the corner swings to the driver's right.

Some of the Scandinavians, particularly the great theorist Rauno Aaltonen, have some remarkable ideas about left foot braking with rear-wheel drive. The technique can be applied to work in this case for the front of the car—a stab on the brakes causing the front wheels to lock, which can be used to alter the attitude of the car in a slide. Rauno also has a theory that if you give a stab on the brakes just before you set the car up for the corner this can tweak-up the suspension of certain cars into a more taut attitude. This, I suspect, may be one of the little Finn's ideas that don't actually work, but he hopes that you'll try to master them!

Generally, I would recommend that you leave left foot braking to the experts and it is certainly not a technique to be practised in your Austin 1100 on a greasy roundabout on the Guildford by-pass! Remember, it can only be done properly if you are travelling really fast on dirt roads and in a car that is properly set-up for competition work.

Ditch hooking

One of the tricks of the trade in high-speed forestry driving is to use to the best advantage the cambers and ditches on the inside of corners. If there is a good camber on the inside obviously it's only sensible to make the best use of it. Much the same effect can be achieved by hooking the front wheels into the gully or the ditch on the inside. You should however, keep a wary eye out for logs or big rocks because these can easily throw you off line or, worse still, damage the suspension.

The forestry roads, however, generally run to some sort of pattern and it is always worthwhile when you enter a forest, and when you are driving along the not-so-difficult stretches, to try and get the feel of the land. A fast, smooth road probably has well-drained usable ditches, while a track with big rocks around will probably have equally rough ditches.

Brows

Blind brows are among the most dangerous hazards that the rally driver has to face. Again, it's worthwhile trying to sum up the character of the forest as you drive along and this may give you some guide as to which way the unseen road may turn. But this information should only be logged in your mind as a hunch and it would be foolish not to treat every brow with respect.

Just as you want to get the car into an unbalanced attitude before an unknown corner, so that you may be in a position to take the necessary action when you can see the severity of the corner, so it is wise to try and arrive at the crest of a brow with the car travelling slightly sideways, to the left or to the right according to your previous hunch. As you pass over the brow you are then at least able to take three courses of action.

If the road is straight you can quickly correct the slide and accelerate. If the road turns towards the direction in which you have the car set up then you are already in the best position to take that corner. If the road turns in the opposite direction then, by over-correcting your original slide, you can very quickly have the car set up and pointing the right way.

When the car takes off on a brow (sometimes called 'yumping') try and land as straight as possible to avoid undue damage to the suspension and steering. Lift off the throttle at the point of take-off to avoid over-revving and be ready to accelerate hard when you land.

Bumps

The same technique should be applied to bumps that you hit with one wheel; again it is very important to try and hit them straight and in a position when the steering and suspension are best set up to receive the blow. For deep gulleys across the road, however, that you will hit with all four wheels, it is worthwhile trying to cross them at an angle to lessen the shock. Always try and get your braking over before you hit the bump for you will probably do more damage to the car if you hit the hazard with locked wheels. With Minis, particularly those with Hydrolastic suspension, it is worthwhile stamping on the throttle just before you hit the hazard for this tends to lift the car up a little, which could make just the difference between a whole and a holed sump!

If the car is thrown sideways on a bump you may start to fishtail upon landing. This should be controlled by getting the car steering straight first and then bringing in the power to pull it into line.

Mud and water

There seems to be no special technique for getting out of a muddy situation, for conditions are often variable. It is worthwhile trying different techniques because conditions can change quite dramatically within a small muddy patch, and what did not work a few yards further back might work now. Sometimes the trials method of blipping the throttle all the time keeps the car going, sometimes you are better off with a steady flat-out throttle, sometimes you'll get through with the minimum of acceleration. As momentum is the main objective, if you unexpectedly come across a muddy patch and it does not look as though it goes on for too long, it is best not to hesitate but to build up maximum speed and plough straight on, with the hope that this will carry you through. If you cannot see the firm going on the other side then it is probably worthwhile being a little more cautious.

A useful tip is to see where the water lies on the road. If there is a puddle adjoining a muddy patch it could mean that the ground underneath is harder and that the water has not drained away. On the other hand, it could mean that the water is a lot deeper in the puddle and you would do better to try your luck in the mud!

In tackling deep water the secret is always to go in slowly so that the bow wave does not swamp the engine. It is worthwhile almost stopping, engaging first gear to maintain steady progress, and perhaps even slipping the clutch to keep the revs up.

Dust and fog

These are really beastly hazards and again there is no special technique. When you are following and trying to pass another competitor in the dust it is always better to try and get as close to him as possible so that you are driving in advance of the dust cloud. You are then in a better position to keep up with him which, if you are in a slower car, will be an advantage and, if you can overtake, you will be in a better position to spot an opportunity. When you do go past and the road is wide enough it may be worthwhile trying to pass up wind to avoid the dust cloud.

There is no special technique for driving in fog but it can be helpful if you sit a little closer to the screen in really bad conditions. Certainly you should always keep the screen wipers going, with adequate lubrication from the screen washers. Driving on fog lamps alone is always preferable to dipped main beams as it cuts down the back glare. Despite the Frenchmen's addiction to yellow lights there is no scientific proof that these reduce glare or give better performance in fog. Unless you are one of those incredible people like Simo Lampinen who have some sort of sixth sense about seeing through the fog, you are best advised to lose time rather than scare the hell out of your co-driver!

Before you take a chance on passing another competitor in a blind situation it is worthwhile trying to get the feel of the road before you make the all-important decision. If you have just been through a twisty section with unexpected narrow stretches, perhaps with bridges, you are obviously better to wait until the pattern of the road improves to wider and straighter conditions.

Overtaking a slower competitor, even when visibility is good, can be difficult on a confined forestry track. Baulking is very frustrating for a faster driver and, although most drivers are very good at moving over, there are one or two who need a little persuasion to let you through!

There is no real technique other than to indicate to the fellow in front that you are travelling a whole lot faster than he is. You should try and catch him up quickly and get right on his tail. If you hang back and wait for the opportunity to pass he may only have time to catch an occasional glimpse of you in his mirror and he may well think that he's able to match your pace. Besides, if you are close up with him you'll be able to squirt past quickly when the situation is right, which will cause the minimum of delay to you both.

Rallymanship

Not the least important aspect of rally driving is the art of rallymanship, and the need to keep yourself in the right state of mind for the job in hand. Pacing your performance and effort over a long-distance event is the hardest thing to learn and is the hallmark of the true professional. But you can practise this on even a small club rally by switching off and relaxing on the easy road sections. This is the time when you can also save your car by reducing the rev limits, going easy on the brakes and making less hurried gear changes. It could be that your co-driver can take the wheel here and it is worthwhile exhausting a number of candidates for the hot seat until you find the most suitable combination.

Everyone will get tired at some point during a rally but this is not dangerous in itself. What is important is that you learn to be the firm judge of how tired you are and whether the time has come when you must hand over the wheel. With practice you'll learn to sleep in the car and it is surprising how even a five-minute nap at a control can restore your morale. Eating is a matter of personal preference, but most people find that if you have 20 minutes to spare a light meal is more beneficial than sleep.

But, above all, and far more important than being able to perform the manoeuvres that we have described, is the will to win or, for the less skilled, the will to finish. The man who is able to brush aside all problems and keep on trying will not only achieve success in the events that he enters, but if he applies that determination to his general approach to rallying he stands a very good chance of achieving his ambitions.

CHAPTER 2

Conform by numbers

Hamish Cardno, rally contributor to 'Motor', investigates the thorny subject of homologation

IN THE BEGINNING (well, almost) there were rallies and other forms of motoring sport, and the best combination of crew and car won, and everybody was happy. Then the people who made the car realised that if it had won something this might be an impressive fact with which to sway prospective customers, so the manufacturers started to publicise their victories. Logically, their next step was to make sure that they won. They employed the best crews to drive the cars, and they introduced service—but even that wasn't always enough.

The manufacturers started to improve the cars, and that was the end of the beginning, or the beginning of the end, if you prefer. Because they realised that although the Slugmobile was a very good car, and quite good enough for the average customer, it would go much faster and therefore stand a much greater chance of victory if fitted with a Franticlia engine, which had 50 per cent more power. (If this were a true story the manufacturers would then find that on the first special stage the extra power would snap the drive shafts but it isn't, so never mind.)

The Sluglia was a very successful car, and the more events it won the more and more the manufacturers advertised its successes, and their sales graphs knew no bounds. But the average customer was becoming disgruntled (and the authorities of motoring sport disturbed) because it was perfectly obvious that the Slugmobile in the showroom was not good enough to win a local treasure hunt, let alone the Monte Carlo Rally. Only then did he notice the little asterisk on the ad which proclaimed: 'Slugmobile wins Monte—again', and saw that opposite another asterisk at the bottom of the page it said 'Class 45, subdivision 39', which (had the average buyer access to the regulations for the event) meant that the winning car was about as closely related to his purchase as a Boeing 747 is to a Tiger Moth.

The situation was clearly unsatisfactory in two ways. As the above fairy story attempts to point out, the customer had no idea whether the 'winning car' he had bought bore any relation to the actual winning car, and also because the more modifications that were made to a car the more expensive it became. This meant that the wealthiest company (in theory, at any rate) would win every time, and a poor company could not afford to be even competitive. Homologation is an attempt to overcome both problems, though whether it does is a matter for argument.

The word comes from the Greek 'homos', meaning 'the same' (a fact of startlingly little relevance to this article, but you can pick up a classical education in the most unlikely places). You can't make all cars the same, of course, but what the present rules do is to limit the differences.

But first a word about where the rules come from. The world's governing body of motoring sport is the Fédération Internationale de l'Automobile (FIA for short), which has its headquarters in Paris and operates rather like the United Nations. It is concerned in the politics of motoring, is made up of representatives from leading motoring organisations in various countries (the RAC in Great Britain), and isn't necessarily united.

Its most controversial subsidiary is the Commission Sportive Internationale (CSI), to which the member organisations send representatives who, in their view, are their country's greatest experts on sporting matters. If I appear slighting about the membership of the CSI it is because (as in many other organisations) the people who have the time and the inclination to do such a job are frequently one step (or two) removed from what they purport to represent, and this is sometimes reflected in their decisions. It is also because, for an organisation which governs the actions of a large number of people and which makes very far-reaching decisions affecting the livelihoods of these people, its communications seem poor.

The CSI in turn has a technical sub-committee, composed of six of its membership, and this meets four times a year to consider applications for homologation. The applications are in Groups, established under a set of rules known as Appendix J. It is an appendix to the Sporting Code of the CSI; the Sporting Code sets out the general rules for running motoring sport, Appendix J details the mechanical specifications.

Rallying with standard production cars is not very popular in England but the Group 1 category has a strong following in Europe. Opel in particular have been consistently successful with the Rallye Kadett.

CONFORM BY NUMBERS

Appendix J groups for rally cars

Group 1

Series Production Touring Cars
Minimum annual production 5000 cars
- BMW 2002 TI
- Opel Commodore GS
- Renault Gordini R8
- Opel Rallye Kadett
- Citroen DS 21
- Wartburg

when modified become
↓

Group 2

Special Touring Cars
Minimum annual production 1000 cars
- BMW 2002 TI
- Alfa Romeo GT/AM
- Opel Rallye Kadett
- Mini-Cooper S
- Ford Escort Twin Cam
- Ford Escort RS 1600
- Saab V4

Group 3

Series Production Grand Touring Cars
Minimum annual production 1000 cars
- Porsche 911 S
- Alfa-Romeo Spider

when modified become
↓

Group 4

Special Grand Touring Cars
Minimum annual production 500 cars
- Alpine-Renault 1600
- Porsche 914/6
- Lancia 1600 HF
- Fiat 124 Spider

when further modified become
↓

Group 5/6*

Prototype cars
No minimum annual production
- Ford GT 70
- Simca CG-MC
- Most club rally cars
- Marathon and World Cup Rally cars

*Table showing the homologated groups of cars for rallying. The models shown are those that are currently the most regular entries in each group. *The present Groups 5 and 6 are shortly to be amalgamated.*

In formulating technical regulations the CSI is advised by another international organisation, the Bureau Permanent Internationale des Constructeurs Automobile (BPICA) on which Great Britain is represented through the Society of Motor Manufacturers and Traders (SMM and T).

Appendix J was introduced early in 1957, ran concurrently with the old mechanical rules (Appendix C) for a couple of years, and has been on its own since then. So have a lot of people trying to understand it.

By definition, a set of rules detailing limitations on modifications to something as complex as the modern motor car must be lengthy, and as there is no room for ambiguity they tend to be as verbose and turgid as most legal documents. A working knowledge of them is essential for any competition manager or competitor, and in addition most factories with an interest in motoring sport have a tame expert whose responsibility is to see that the correct parts are homologated for each model.

The actual homologation document for one car is formidable. When a manufacturer wants his car approved, a form detailing the dimensions of every part—plus photographs of the car and some of the components—has to be completed, in triplicate. He then sends it to the RAC Motor Sport Division, whose Director, Mr Dean Delamont, is Britain's representative on the CSI and chairman of the CSI's technical sub-committee. The forms arrive on the desk of Neil Eason-Gibson, an amiable, studious-looking young man who is more or less a walking encyclopaedia of facts about cars and motoring sport. His job is to check the application, to make sure that the form is correctly filled-in, and that the facts on it are accurate and true.

'People don't cheat now, although at one time one or two people used to try and slip something through,' he says. 'You occasionally find something which seems a bit odd, and it's usually quite easy to check up on it. We had an application in for a car last year on which the weight figure seemed a bit low. We checked and found it was more than 1 cwt lighter than it should have been, told the people concerned and they changed it.'

In fact, the safeguards which the FIA (and the RAC as its agents) can take against cheating are considerable. If the FIA suspects that, say, the weight of a car looks odd, it can go to the production line of the factory, or to a number of dealers, remove five cars at random, weigh them, and homologate the car at the average weight of the five. The FIA does check up on things anyway, by sending one of the members of the technical sub-committee to a factory or its competitions department to inspect a car or a number of parts and ensure that cheating isn't taking place. As a safeguard against patriotism, a member from another country is also sent, so that if for example a French manufacturer had something which needed checking, the French member of the committee would go to the factory, accompanied by a representative from another country.

'One of our main problems is getting the people concerned to send things in on time,' says Eason-Gibson. 'The meetings are held in March, June, September and December, and the forms have to be with us well before then to be checked, sent to Paris, copied and checked again, and then approved by the meeting for the homologation to take effect from the first day of the following month. People sometimes don't get the forms to us on time, and sometimes—particularly when there are strikes—they have not made a sufficient number of cars or parts for approval by the time of the meeting. There is a procedure to accommodate this sort of thing. We can put the proposal forward and say that the expected number should be made by a certain date, then we check that this has been done by that date.'

Looking at the paperwork involved, one can understand even the tame experts getting into trouble with it. The application form itself runs to 12 pages and must include 17 photographs per form showing different views of the car, and detail shots—combustion

If you can't beat 'em join 'em. Above: The rally car that everyone was trying to beat in 1971—the Group 4 Alpine-Renault 1600. Below: Ford's challenge for the 1972 season, the GT70. While manufacturers with big competition budgets can afford to build these specialised models, designed primarily to win rallies, there are many who feel that a return to competition between more standard touring cars would be both less expensive and more attractive to the public.

chamber, piston crown, inlet and exhaust manifolds—plus drawings of various engine parts. Then there are all the dimensions to be filled-in, pages of them. The English language instructions on filling-in the form run to nine pages alone, again written in the sort of legalese which leaves one's mind boggling by its verbosity. To give an example:

Art 9, sub-section a—engines. 'Should a same coachwork model be available with several engines of different power and/or cylinder-capacity, these engines may be recognised by submitting an additional variant form, provided the cylinder-capacities of the different engines remain within the same engine-capacity class (see art 252 of Appendix J) and provided the manufacturer supplies for each version certificate of minimum production of the same order as that given for the basic model. Moreover, on the basic form of the model concerned, it is the engine of the lowest power and/or cylinder-capacity which must appear.'

In general most rules and regulations, particularly those in sports which are still predominantly amateur, suffer from a tendency to call a spade an implement with a metal blade and wooden handle which is inserted into the ground at an angle near the vertical and then swung through an axis of some 30 degrees before it is lifted from the ground, taking some of the earth with it. If you see what I mean.

In this respect the homologation rules are probably no worse than many and better than some. Rally regulations could be quite baffling, and although they have improved greatly in recent years, disputes can still arise over loose wording.

But I digress. Simplification has been a working motto so far as even Appendix J is concerned for several years, and real progress has been made. While Formula 1 racing cars have become more and more way out and closer to spacecraft than motor cars, the trend is for rally cars to become closer to the showroom model.

Of the Groups under which a car can be homologated, only the first six could conceivably venture into anything remotely like a rally (see accompanying table). Group 6 cars can be real prototypes like the Ford GT70, or they can be cars of more mundane origin which have been modified to such an extent that they can no longer be considered similar to production cars. A great many cars used for club rallying in Britain fall into this category, particularly those built for special stage rallying which have been strengthened far more than the rules for the other groups would permit.

Group 5 sports cars are rare birds in international rallying as well. Cars like the Porsche 917 come into this category and it is only on events such as the Tour de France, where the road mileage is of slight importance and the results are decided on performance in races and hill-climbs, that they appear. However, if some brave soul wants to use a Porsche 917 in the Tour of Eppynt, I'm sure a very large crowd will turn out to watch his progress— from a safe distance.

All cars which take part in rallies in the Manufacturers' section of the European Rally Championship must come from the first four Groups. Group 4 cars are devices such as the Alpine-Renault 1600 and the Porsche 914/6, of which 500 must be made in a year to qualify. These are the real 'fliers' when conditions suit them, and when you reckon the sort of power and handling combination which could be dreamed up by a designer with a large budget, and produced in such a (relatively) small number, you realise why Ford have embarked on the GT70 project.

Group 3 cars—such as the Alpine-Renault 1300, which uses the R8 Gordini engine, and the Porsche 911S—are the sports cars which are bought by the public. The manufacturers have to produce 1,000 of these per year to qualify, and although these were the 'racers' of the rally world a couple of years ago, as manufacturers have invested more and more money in striving for success they have been displaced by cars in Group 4.

Until January 1970 there were two groups for modified touring cars (a touring car, by the way, is a four-seater: a Capri qualifies, a 911S does not, which just shows how careful coupé designers have to be about the amount of room they provide in the back). Touring cars could be Group 2, which basically meant slightly modified, or the old Group 5, which meant very much modified.

Since then Groups 2 and 5 have been combined into Group 2, although there is this very serious restriction that 1,000 cars a year have to be built to qualify. Works saloon cars such as the Ford Escort Twin-Cam and the Saab V4 are Group 2 cars, and although one might think it reasonably easy to make a Twin-Cam, ensure it works, produce 1,000 and go and win rallies in this category, life is never as simple as it seems.

A great deal of freedom—particularly to the wealthier competitors—is permitted by a clause which states that all manner of things will be allowed, provided 100 of them are made and are available for fitting to 100 cars. Under this heading come most of the things done by the works, which explains why their cars are so much better than those of the private entrants—limited-slip differentials, five-speed gearboxes, dry-sump lubrication systems, cylinder heads of different design and different material, different transmission shafts and half shafts. The same number of 'one-offs' have to be available when a modification for a Group 4 car is proposed.

Most arguments about homologation stem from this, and both sides have a very valid case. The FIA view is that a manufacturer must make these available so that he is not producing a different semi-prototype for each event, and so that there is (in theory, at any rate) an opportunity for the private entrant to benefit from the development work of the competitions department.

This has brought about the formation of departments such as the British Leyland Special Tuning Department and Ford's Advanced Vehicles Organisation which manufacture and market homologated parts for the general public to buy.

Critics of this ruling argue that the development work and the production of parts in such small numbers is so costly that only those manufacturers with vast budgets can remain competitive. And they quote this as a reason for the demise of competitions departments such as British Leyland's—or at least cite it as a contributory factor. As I said, there are strong arguments on both sides, and if there is a fair solution I'm sure the authorities of motoring sport would be delighted to hear of it.

They have fewer problems with Group 1 cars, your actual straight-out-of-the-show-room, 5,000 a year production version, mainly because very few people want to rally such a thing (a sad reflection on the quality of the current production car?) and partly because as soon as any obvious modification is made the car becomes Group 2—remove the carpets at your peril!

And the future? Neil Eason-Gibson thinks the current Groups are about as simple as they can get.

'We now have four basic sorts of competition car. The saloon cars—Groups 1 and 2; the sports cars in Groups 3 and 4; and the hybrids in Groups 5 and 6; plus the racing cars in Groups 7, 8 and 9. I don't think we'll alter that basic formula for some time except that Groups 5, 6 and 7 are now becoming the happy hunting ground of the two-seater 'racers' and might as well be lumped together under one heading. There have been loopholes in the regulations, but as soon as they are spotted they are closed. The system seems to be working well.'

Perhaps it is significant that not so very long ago someone thought that the only safe way of getting round the regulations was having his own homologation forms printed—and did!

CHAPTER 3

Some like it hot

Doug Watts, former supervisor of the BMC and British Leyland Competitions Department, gives some expert advice on rally car preparation

---

THE OLD SAYING that 'to win you must first finish' applies more to rallying than to any other branch of motoring sport. How often on rallies have we seen someone come through to win on reliability rather than out-and-out performance? And so often silly little faults put a car out of a rally. I have seen a man spend a fortune on fitting the hottest camshaft in his engine and then retire because he forgot to fit the cheapest rubber grommet to protect the headlight wiring where it passed through the bulkhead. It's no use having the fastest car in the event if you cannot see where you are going!

Before we start on the business of car preparation I assume that the reader is familiar with the rules and regulations of the sport. If not, then I suggest that you go to the RAC and buy a copy of the RAC Motor Sport Year Book (the Blue Book) which will tell you all you want to know about the British club events. If you are going international then you must have a copy of the FIA Year Book. The subject of homologation is well expounded by Hamish Cardno in a later chapter in this Rally Manual.

Whatever type of event you enter do study the regulations carefully in respect of what you can and cannot do to the car. There is nothing more futile than spending a lot of money on a certain modification, travelling 2,000 miles to the start of a continental event and then being excluded at scrutineering!

At this point an outline of the modifications permitted within the different groups is called for. Of necessity this must be brief and with the rules being amended regularly the only true references are the Appendix J regulations and the homologation forms which you can obtain from the RAC.

Group 1—Series production touring cars

Modifications are not permitted to engine, transmission, suspension or body parts, neither is reboring allowed. Lights may be added up to a maximum of six. The jets may be changed in the carburettors, as may the battery or generator. Spark plugs, coils, condenser, distributor and voltage control regulator are free (ie the choice is yours), together with the shock absorbers, but alterations are not permitted to the shock absorber mountings.

Tyres are free but the wheels must be standard or optional equipment manufactured in sufficient quantity to permit homologation. Brake and clutch lining materials are free, but it is not permitted to fit larger-area pads or linings. The braking system may be modified to dual circuit as long as you use a cylinder by the same manufacturer. You cannot fit a special seat, but you can add a seat cover to shape it. You cannot fit quick-release buttons to the grille or bonnet fastening, and bumpers must remain.

As you can see, while you may strip and reassemble the power unit very carefully, you may not add to or change any part from its normal material, weight or dimensions. Outright winners do not come from this category so the manufacturers tend to stick to Group 2 or 6 entries which makes the Group 1 class a good one for the private owner. As the regulations are so strictly governed the emphasis is on driver capability and careful preparation for reliability.

Group 2—Special touring cars

Immediately you add anything to your Group 1 car that is not permitted it is automatically transferred to this category or, if extensively modified, you must run in Group 6 (see later).

In Group 2 the stroke may not be altered but a rebore is permitted up to the limit of the cylinder capacity of the class (ie 1,275 cc Cooper 'S' + .020 inch gives 1,293 cc, but a + .040 inch rebore would take it to 1,311 cc and not be permitted). Any parts may be changed as long as they are the same material; you could not, for instance, replace a normal En17 crankshaft with an En50 nitrided type (which is why the Cooper 'S' had a nitrided one as standard).

All manifolds are free but you cannot fit fuel injection unless it is available as a standard option. The position, driving system and number of camshafts is fixed but in every other way camshafts are free, along with valve gear.

The gearbox is virtually free but you may not alter the number of speeds available; all rear axle or final drive ratios are free. Limited-slip differentials may be added provided they fit the axle without modification, but you may not lock the differential entirely. All springs are free but not their mountings; this applies to every spring in the car. Stabiliser

The private owner has a multitude of competition parts from which to choose but it's best to buy from the works. These are some of the competition parts sold for the Mini-Cooper 'S' by the British Leyland Special Tuning Department.

Reliability must be the aim for the privateer and as far as engine preparation is concerned this is best achieved by the careful assembly of the standard unit rather than extravagant modifications.

bars, normally referred to as anti-roll bars, may be added, together with additional locating arms to the axles such as Panhard rods or torsion bars. Steering ratio is free.

Wheels are free in respect of diameter and rim width, but all wheels must be of the same diameter. However, they must not protrude outside the bodywork or wing extensions, the wing extensions being limited to a 5 cm maximum increase per side on wing width.

All electrical equipment is free and you may, for instance, replace a dynamo with an alternator to increase the output. The battery location is free. The radiator is free, as are the oil cooler and fuel tanks, which may be enlarged up to the maximum permitted for the cylinder capacity class. The braking equipment is free but the actual friction areas may not be altered. Servos may be added, as can cooling ducts, provided they do not entail body modifications.

Lightened body parts are allowed as options but they are not permitted to alter the standard homologated weight. Roll cages must now be installed in Group 2 cars but the weight of the structure must be added to the homologation form and to the normal weight recognised.

Safety factors affect Group 2 cars in other ways. Fire extinguishers must be carried and the FIA now insists on a dry powder type of at least 1 kilogram capacity. Safety fuel cells are compulsory for Groups 2, 4, 5 and 6, while optional for 1 and 3. These are usually reinforced rubber tanks, foam-filled, the foam being a special product to a critical specification and very expensive. Some tanks are built in steel or alloy with a rubber bag insert.

Irrespective of Group, safety belts should be fitted, while laminated windscreens are insisted on for all competition, together with bonnet and boot lid locking devices or straps. You may cover any exposed pipes or cable under the car with a metal shield and you must shield any internal fuel pipe. All engine breathers should be collected to a suitable catch tank of 2 litre capacity for vehicles up to 2,000 cc and of 3 litre capacity for vehicles over 2,000 cc.

Group 3—Series production grand touring cars

The modifications permitted are the same as those for Group 1 cars.

Group 4—Special grand touring cars

For these small-production performance cars the modifications permitted are the same as for Group 2. It follows that any Group 3 car can be modified into Group 4 but a Group 2 car is not eligible for either.

Group 5—Sports cars

These high-performance cars are not usually catered for in rallies so there is little point in discussing this category.

Group 6—Prototype cars

This is the most potent category catered for in rallies and it is governed only by safety and common sense. The car must have normal equipment for public roads. It can be an open car and there is no stipulation as to minimum weight, but fuel tank capacity has

A roll-over bar to the new FIA specifications is now required for all international events. Its dimensions, construction and attachment to the chassis are clearly laid down.

limits for differing engine capacities. This is the manufacturer's playground for prototype components and experiments, the field of the one-off models built to win. The private owner should leave it to the works boffins!

Two important things arise from the above, both taking effect from January 1972. The cars of existing Groups 5 and 6 will be amalgamated as new Group 5 sports cars with no minimum production, but weight limits are introduced for the differing engine capacities as they exist for current Group 5 cars, with some alteration. The lightweight panels and Plexiglass windows which are currently on Group 2/4 homologation forms will no longer be recognised from that date and it will not be possible to introduce such options.

Now that you have some idea of what you can and cannot do within the various regulations, we come down to the more practical advice on carrying out the work of preparation. For Sunday afternoon social runs and the smaller club night rallies you are not going to need any radical modifications, for the brilliance of your navigator will probably be more important than the choice of a differential or a camshaft profile! An accurate speedometer, good driving lights, a map reading light and careful attention to detail when you do your normal maintenance jobs are all that is required.

When club rallying becomes your hobby, rather than an occasional weekend excuse to take the girl friend out for a spin, the choice of car and its preparation becomes rather more significant. The manufacturers who have concentrated for a time on rallying a particular model will probably be your first choice. They will have homologated a range of special parts which will be available for sale through their general trade outlets. Although fortunes ebb and flow in international competition, the manufacturers that have proved themselves successful at one time or another must offer the best choice of a suitable rally car.

Common sense dictates that you will go Group 1 in internationals or Group 2 if you can afford it. Preparation to be competitive in restricted events will be nearer Group 2, but this does not prevent many competitors thoroughly enjoying themselves with well-prepared road cars.

The small-budget man will do well to prepare his car to Group 1 standards for you cannot introduce engine modifications so it is a case of making certain that you are getting the best from what there is. Check all suspension mountings, exhaust pipe clamps, brake pipes and fuel lines. Be certain that all flexible fuel pipes are effectively clipped in place. Fancy instruments are pointless, but the speedometer should be accurately calibrated and gauges are better than warning lights. Examine the condition of the wiring, for so much depends on tidy, clean recognisable wiring.

Bodywork

Moving on to the preparation of a more competitive car for rougher road events, ideally you should start with the bare bodyshell. In normal production the major panels are brought together and spot-welded, quite satisfactorily for all normal purposes but not for rough rally treatment. These seams should now be carefully welded, ideally electrically, by feathering. Panels which are highly stressed (supports for suspension mountings, etc) should be double-skinned with mild steel sheet. All tie bar mountings should be gusseted. Turret mountings, like the top of the Escort/Cortina MacPherson struts, take a terrific pounding and should also be double-skinned.

The suspension loads of a Mini are taken by the sub-frames. These should be removed and the top of each turret welded all round. Side members should be double-skinned and each tie bar mounting gusseted. A lot of twist takes place along the front member, so use the export sump shield in heavy gauge steel, bolted firmly at the sides and at intervals along the front. Carefully check the front bulkhead, sealing unnecessary holes; this must

The most important fitting for rough road work is a sump guard. These are available from the works for most popular models.

form an effective firewall. Now is the time to introduce your own instrument layout and dash panelling, and commence the wiring scheme.

Engine mounting brackets should be strengthened, together with double-skinning the radiator brackets. If the radiator is engine-mounted (like the Mini) discard these brackets entirely and mount it directly on the body panel. The floor panel takes a hefty torsional load and it is wise to strengthen this along the tunnel section. A roll cage is mandatory for most events but do not waste time attempting to make one yourself. Regulations state the specification of material, tube diameter and thickness. The only safe answer is to get one from a specialist, like John Aley. Mounting points for the roll cage must be reinforced by steel plates at least 3/32 inch thick, welded or bolted in position.

The brake pipes, fuel lines, battery cables, Hydrolastic pipes, etc, can now be routed through the shell, clipped at regular intervals, and run along the sills where clumsy feet will not crush them. The fuel pipe should always be metal tube or armoured, never plastic.

If the car originally has a pistol grip handbrake you should investigate the adaptation of a centre, or side fitting type, made to 'fly-off'. As these are invariably cable-operated it is a case of deciding the position, fabricating a strong mounting bracket and adapting the cable and its supports to the rear linkage.

If the battery is normally in the front engine compartment it can be moved to the back with advantage, getting it away from the heat and moving the weight to the back. A strong box framework can be fitted in the boot but it must leave the battery accessible. Do not tuck it in a corner, and be sure to shield the terminals. More than one fire has been caused by a spanner floating around in the boot.

It is recommended that an isolation switch be fitted externally, in addition to the internal ignition control. Common practice is to break the earth lead from the battery but this is useless as it has no effect when the engine is running. The circuit broken must include the charging cable from the voltage regulator to battery (ie not the earth side, irrespective of positive or negative system).

While in the boot, the fuel pump should be securely mounted, preferably high, where things cannot roll on to it and short-circuit the electrics. The type of pump is very important; it should be the SU AUF 400 series with dual electrics but common fuel connections. With the old regulations it was necessary for the electric terminal to be moved physically from one end of the pump to the second terminal at the other end, but there is nothing to prevent them both being wired to a two-position switch now, though you should never have both running together. Alternatively, the slightly higher rate, solid state type of pumps by Bendix or Mitsuba can be twinned with the same result, but these are more expensive.

Fuel tank capacity is important and a safety type is the only sane choice, like those from FPT of Bournemouth or Marston of Wolverhampton—expensive but worth every penny. If auxiliary tanks are fitted make sure the pumps feed from the lowest tank. The filler cap is best left attached to the tank so you must open the boot lid unless there is an orifice in the boot lid. Standard tanks in many models are located underneath at the rear. Exposed to damage, they are best discarded. Similarly, fillers that protrude can be damaged in an accident, leaking fuel or splitting the tank. A securely clamped tank breather pipe should be taken outside to the roof channelling, terminating in a 'U' to prevent ingress of water. The rear bulkhead must be sealed to make it a firewall and prevent the entry of liquids.

Any floor holes where accessories or seat brackets have been removed should be brazed over or sealed. Carry out a careful search for these, as exhaust fumes all night long are dangerous. Nobody is perfect, so reinforce the shell at front and rear to fit towing eyes, and strong jacking points should be welded in position at the front, rear and at each side. These can be useful when deditching, or in deep mud when the car can be jacked up and pushed sideways off the jack.

The windscreen must be laminated. Unless you intend to do extensive continental rallying the cost of a heated version is prohibitive and increases the load on the generator. Rear and side windows can be in Plexiglass (minimum thickness 4 mm) to save weight, but remember the earlier comment about 1972 regulations. Lightweight body panels are also subject to the 1972 amendment, although this does not affect the club entrant. The choice is glass fibre or alloy panels, in some cases as skin on metal frames. With these items you must ensure that the hinges, strikers, locks, etc, are mounted in reinforced areas with large support washers. Doors must shut and lock securely. Bonnet internal releases are a nuisance and if possible the pull control cable should be shortened so that it may be operated through the front grille. In addition, safety catches should be added, either straps or the lug and pin type. For quickness the boot catch can be dispensed with and two safety catches used.

Suspension

All suspension components must be retained with castellated nuts, pinned or lock-wired; in other cases use Nyloc type nuts at least. Rubber bushed joints for shackles etc, are best replaced with harder types or Timken bearings. Normal ones are often squeezed right out by the pounding taken on a rough rally. All suspension arms, front hubs and steering arms should be crack-tested or replaced with special heat-treated components.

Roller and ball bearings are manufactured to very high quality with little to choose between them so do not take chances with hub or shaft bearing surfaces and always take

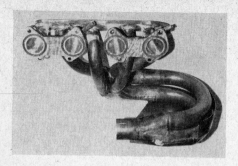

Rally manifold with skid guard for an Imp.   *Rear suspension bump stop kit for an 1800.*

Weber carburettor kit for the BMC 'A' series   *Rubber fuel tank, with twin electrical pumps*
engine.   *for a Mini.*

care when fitting a bearing to prevent damage to the surfaces. Steering arms should be scrupulously clean for fitting, preferably with any mating surfaces or tapers ground in.

A high ratio steering rack or box should be fitted where possible. Various anti-roll or stabiliser bars are available and the advice of your particular manufacturer is best sought. The actual rate will be dependent on the spring rates, shock absorber stiffness and wheel weight chosen.

Uprated shock absorbers or struts are a must. The standard Cooper 'S' already has the stiff rate displacer units, and other models can change entirely to the Cooper 'S' system (ie displacers, springs and struts). Adjustable shock absorbers are ideal and these can also be fitted additionally to the front of Hydrolastic Minis. The shock absorber stroke must be greater than the suspension travel or it becomes a 'checkstrap' overloading its brackets.

Spring rates are very important, again uprated units are available for most models. We do not want stiff race types, as we must also increase the travel and raise the ride height, but not too much as this will increase the roll centre. This also means that suspension arms and drive shafts will move through wider arcs than intended so the answer is to use larger progressive bump rebound rubbers, as available from Aeon for instance. These prevent the shafts 'necking' and oversize bump rubbers are handy spares to get you home should the suspension fail.

Axle shafts should be in uprated material and, together with drive shafts, be heat-treated and crack-tested. On the Imp models stronger drive shafts and drive 'doughnuts' are a must. Where mountings are bolted in position or tie rods clamped, it is well worth increasing the retaining bolt to the next larger size by drilling out.

Brakes

When fitting the brake assemblies to the hubs, careful attention must be paid to the run of flexible hoses. The hoses should at all times be covered with ¾ inch diameter coils of thin piano wire to protect from stones. Similarly the bundy tubes running from backplate to flexible hose connection on the axle or swinging arm must be protected with a length of rubber pipe, split to fit over and then bound with sealing tape. If a brake pipe has an exposed run beneath a swinging arm it should be modified to run above or a channel section bracket made up to protect it. The brake backing plates can have a number of holes drilled at the bottom to allow water to escape quickly.

Disc brake assemblies have dust covers for normal use. It is advisable to trim these back or remove them altogether, but this does increase the risk of scored discs. The distinct advantage is in allowing air to the discs and greatly increased cooling, a very important factor on a rally car. The old covers can often be modified into ducts to increase the air flow to the disc with even better benefits. Special brake materials are able to withstand much higher temperatures effectively. Ferodo DS11 for pads and VG 95 (a woven asbestos and brass wire material) for linings are the most popular. On the Imp, with its all-drum system, you would use VG 95 at the front with AM3 at the rear. In considering the problem of overheated brake fluid, and possible total loss of brakes, great steps have been taken to counteract this. Castrol Girling Brake Fluid, for instance, does not vapourise until extremely high temperatures so this or an alternative fluid should be used.

Another important fact to remember is that the fluid is hygroscopic, which means that it absorbs moisture from the atmosphere and must be kept sealed at all times. Any contamination reduces its efficiency. Change it often.

The heat generated in the brakes is also increasingly absorbed into the hubs and bearings which is why they must in turn be protected with high melting point greases such as FCB. The biggest single aid to reducing these temperatures has been magnesium wheels, their better ventilation and the natural conductivity of the magnesium alloy dissipate heat away from hubs, brakes and tyres considerably quicker than standard steel disc wheels. Needless to add, the wheels are up to 75 per cent lighter, even with wider rims, which is another advantage in reducing unsprung weight, apart from its inherent strength.

The subject of tyres is best left to the advice of the manufacturers. Leaders in the rally world are Dunlop and Goodyear, with the ever-popular SP44 and Ultragrip Rally Specials as all-rounders and the SP 3/Sport or Grand Prix dual purpose tyres.

Engine

Turning now to engine preparation, the unit should be stripped and all components carefully scrutinised; if in doubt scrap it. This is the only way to ensure as near as possible 100 per cent reliability.

The block must be sound and the cylinder head face surface ground flat. All the core plugs should have their edges peened over. Holes for cylinder head studs should be checked for depth in respect of the stud length and the tops of the stud holes countersunk to prevent lift and gasket failure. Bores must be perfect, or bored/sleeved as required, and correct pistons fitted. The con rods should be crack-tested and polished, pistons being centralised. Before assembly it is wise to bevel the edges of the rod and cap mating faces with a light file. Always use new high-tensile con rod bolts. All rotating and reciprocating parts must be carefully matched and balanced, the crankshaft being done as an assembly with clutch

Electrical troubles have been the cause of countless rally retirements. Attention to detail is well worth while.

pressure plate, flywheel (lightened) and pulley/damper. The solid steel pulley/damper units are preferred to the composite type. The clutch should have increased torque capacity to withstand the increased loadings. When re-assembling, cleanliness is the rule and all friction surfaces should be smeared with an anti-scuffing paste. Gasket surfaces should be coated with a compound like Hylomar, expensive but second to none.

The con rod and main bearing shells are of prime importance; special competition ones have increased clearances for quicker bedding in. It is suggested that the copper-lead-indium type such as Vandervell VP3 are used. Steel main bearing caps are not permitted within Group 2 but are a definite advantage on a three-bearing engine where all torsional whip is taken by the centre main. They should not be necessary on a well-designed five-bearing unit and do present the problem of line boring for oversize bearing shells.

The choice of camshaft must be made with care. It is a waste of time and money to fit a high lift, extended overlap type which results in no power below 3,500 rpm and precious little then until around 5,000 rpm, with peak power at 7,500 rpm or more. Apart from reducing the reliability of all other engine components, the first couple of hill starts will result in a burnt-out clutch. Aim for a cam which gives good mid-range performance and plenty of torque yet still provides some top-end power, (ie the Ford A2, BMC AEG 510 or Rootes 31 for the Imp). Naturally a distributor with matching advance curve should be used. Correct valve clearances are essential.

Where cam followers are fitted these should be carefully selected and assembled using anti-scuffing compound. For rallying it is perhaps better not to use the lightened variety. Push rods can be lightened but never reduce the thrust areas; this also applies to rocker gear.

If an alternative high-pressure or high-capacity oil pump is available then use it, checking it carefully before assembly. Special oil pick-ups to prevent surge are also available;

CASTROL RALLY MANUAL

check that it has not inadvertently been blocked and be absolutely certain that any connections on the suction side are airtight. Do not forget to lockwire the sump plug.

Cylinder heads should give optimum compression, thus requiring high-octane fuel at all times. However, some countries can only provide around 94 octane at best and on events like the World Cup Rally we have encountered local brews claimed to be 82 octane! On these special events provision has to be made for variable ignition to prevent piston damage, while the actual compression has to be limited to around 9.0:1 at the highest. Most efficient engines in tuned form have the optimum between 11.5 and 12.5:1.

The combustion chamber form has a considerable influence here as it controls the flame front of the burning fuel. It can be progressive, efficient and powerful—or instant, causing detonation and damage. Again a 'race' head is no use. Attention to the ports and valve throats is far more important than a high polish.

Combustion chamber shapes are designed to create some turbulence, which assists the low-speed performance and alleged gas flowing only serves to ruin it completely in most

Tools and spares carried on the car should be the minimum to effect a temporary repair. This kit for a works Saab weighs 55 lb and includes such items as shovels, ready-wired distributor head, first-aid kit, crash helmets with intercoms, spare can of fuel, tin of oil, tow rope, wheelbrace, fire extinguisher, warning triangle, rubber de-ditching mats, torches and assorted essential tools. Wearing the aluminium survival blanket is Saab works driver Tom Trana.

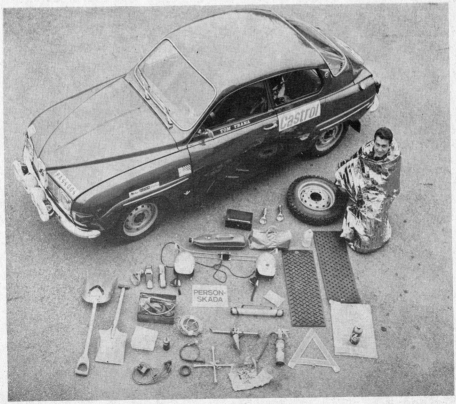

cases. Valve size should not be too large, while springs should prevent surge at peak power without undue load on valve gear or cam. Inlet manifolds should be matched to the head ports with care, including any spacer blocks or gaskets; the carburettor to manifold joint is equally important.

Carburettors come next and the Weber twin-choke is regarded as the most efficient with good reason. An added advantage is that not only the fuel and emulsifying jets enable quick changes, but the actual chokes (the internal throat or venturi) are variable, too. The 45DCOE is familiar to most and this can have from 36 mm to 42 mm chokes, giving a very wide choice. A 1600 cc Twin Cam would use twin 40DCOEs, with 30 chokes and 1.15 main jets, as compared with a single 45DCOE with 38 choke and 1.95 jet on a Cooper 'S', whereas the 998 cc Imp, with its individual inlet ports, would use twin 40DCOEs with 31 mm chokes and 1.20 jets.

Attention must be paid to ensure that the carburettors receive ample clean air. Filtering is essential for rallying. A large capacity duct should incorporate a dust trap before leading to an air box, from which the carburettors breathe. It should be insulated and baffled with air ducted away via a low-pressure area. A closed box can pressurise the air feed at high speed, upsetting the carburation.

The exhaust manifold should be a free-flow multiple branch, mated to the head ports and rigidly constructed with strong brackets to the bell housing. The pipe, silencer and tail pipe should be welded at all joints, with secure brackets for mountings and loose bolts through all rubber mounts. The system should ride as high as possible with plenty of clearance for the rear axle at full bump. Preferably the tail pipe should exit through the rear bottom valance. Each bracket should have a security loop, either a steel strip or a metal braided one so that the exhaust cannot drop off completely. Leading and trailing edges to silencer boxes should have protective skids welded on.

Back to the power unit, all the support brackets for ancillaries such as the generator must be reinforced. It is good policy to clip a new fan belt in position around the timing chain cover for emergencies. A low temperature thermostat should be fitted.

If the engine mounting points have already been strengthened we should now look to the actual mountings. The pounding these receive on rallies can soon shear the rubber completely so alternative harder and shallower angle ones should be fitted. For additional safety these can be drilled through both faces, including the compression medium, then pass a loosely fitted bolt through, lockwiring the nut. This prevents the mounting shearing completely. Do not overlook a tie bar to restrict excessive engine movement from causing damage.

Transmission

Before you rush off for a set of close-ratio gears let's think about what we want from the gearbox. Strength first, so go for straight-cut gears, in stronger material too if available. Ratios are not so easy. Ultra-close-ratio gear sets are useless to the all-rounder, the result will be a spluttering motor, burnt clutch or broken half shaft. Rallying demands are variable, and with a 'torquey' power unit and intermediate uprated gears you will be able to cope with most eventualities.

The current ratios for the four speed synchro Cooper 'S', the Escort Mexico and Imp Sport are a good starting point. The Imp has the advantage with its transaxle and all-indirect variable-ratio gears.

Electrics

Preferably fit an alternator, with separate 4TR regulator, to cope with the demand. All components should be individually wired with separate relays and fuses and preferably

Safari Escort showing the strong bump bar, mesh stone guard over the oil cooler grille, headlamp cleaning wipers, central jacking point and quick-release bonnet catches.

Fully studded SP44 on a Minilite wheel for a Mini. Note the wing extension.

Lightweight bucket driving seat suitable for most British Leyland models.

the fuse boxes should be accommodated on the navigator's dash panel. At all times utilise the services of an expert electrician.

Twin coils should be mounted horizontally or vertically, never at an angle, and in accessible positions. All terminals on the coil, distributor, etc, should have bolted not Lucar connectors. High tension terminals should be coated with silicone grease before the waterproof covers are fitted, and always use the waterproof rubber suppressed spark plug covers. When the ignition system is complete it should be saturated with one of the water repellant sprays on the market. Never guess at spark plugs, give full details to the manufacturers, who will then advise you.

Spot lamps are a matter of personal choice, the conventional wear at the present time being two quartz-iodine spots and two dipped beams. These should be mounted securely on a rigid lamp bar and for added security adjustable support stays to the front body panel will restrict vibration. Cables are best routed through a detachable multi-point plug so that the whole lamp bar can be removed if necessary. Be certain not to restrict the radiator grille area. It is a good idea to fit a fine-mesh screen in front of the radiator and oil cooler matrix to prevent clogging from mud or damage from stones. It must be quickly detachable for cleaning.

Pipes to the oil cooler should be protected with grommets when passing through panels; long runs must be clipped to prevent chafing, but allow for engine movement. The engine will spend a lot of time at high revs, resulting in crankcase compression, therefore ample large-bore breather pipes should be fed from the rocker cover and engine breather to the oil catch tank mentioned previously. The pipes must be securely fixed and clipped.

The importance of comfort is stressed elsewhere but the finishing touches make all the difference. Carpet and trim should be retained for Group 2 events and trim prevents a lot of noise and drumming which can be very tiring. Seats must fit the occupants securely and, with safety belts on, controls must be within easy reach. Brake and clutch pedals can be modified to bring them nearer, and if necessary larger-area pads can be built-up. The accelerator pedal should be strengthened and positioned correctly for heel and toe control.

Never discard the heater for it can be very welcome on a cold night. A good move is to modify the system, increasing the flow to the windscreen and incorporating a fresh-air feed for the crew where it is not provided, with a variable control. Even belted in, the driver tends to get thrown around so a left foot support is wise for the driver and padding on anything within reach.

Effective horns should have a control button centrally on the floor for use by driver or navigator. Similarly the fire extinguisher or Graviner control (a built-in system ducted to engine and fuel tank areas) should be accessible to both crew members.

Last but by no means least we come to the protection of the sump and gearbox. Sump shields are not light (they are made of $\frac{1}{4}$ inch Dural, etc) but they are worth their weight in gold. It should protect the sump with a sponge rubber pad between to prevent stones jamming and chafing through. It should protect the steering arms if possible and extend back to cover the gearbox. Shields are now obtainable in magnesium-alloy, which is costly but gives a considerable weight saving. Pipes should be internal but if you have left them outside (Group 1) then pop rivet thin mild steel plates over them. Plates should also be made up to protect exposed tank wells and battery boxes.

Finally the car should be carefully run-in for 200 or 300 miles, then the final settings for ignition and carburation can be settled on a rolling road where you can simulate operating conditions and tune out any little problems. Avoid at all costs final preparations and tuning on the event!

CHAPTER 4

We're all just a little bit mad!

Jimmy Simpson, of the Castrol Competitions Department, recalls some of the problems of servicing on rallies.

THERE ARE TIMES when we have been out servicing on rallies when I am sure that the locals have considered myself and my colleagues to be quite mad—for example on the 1965 Acropolis Rally.

We stood in silence in the hot Greek sunshine peering down the narrow, dusty road. Timo Makinen and Paul Easter in their Mini-Cooper 'S' who, till now, had looked like winning, were late. The service crews shuffled about hot, tired and more than a little fed-up. And then we heard the unmistakeable whine of a works Mini's straight-cut gears. Seconds later Timo streaked into the service point screaming that there was something drastically wrong with the rear suspension.

'After the control!' yelled Stuart Turner. The Abingdon mechanics flung their neatly laid-out tools and spares into the service car and hurtled off into the village. I ran after them trailing a quick-lift racing jack. My Castrol service car stood where I had left it under the trees, boot, bonnet and doors open.

In the village square, the Mini had already been tipped on to its side. This stunt never failed to both amuse and astonish a crowd and, short of a garage lift or pit, was the simplest way of gaining access to a Mini's underpinnings. The rear sub-frame was damaged and needed welding. By the time the mechanics had everything ready, a considerable amount of fuel had dripped from the vented filler cap, saturating the ground beneath the car. To stem the flow I held a large plastic bag under the leaking filler. About a quart of petrol had collected in the bag when, with a roar and a searing flash, the bag disappeared before my eyes. A blob of white-hot welding rod had dropped on to the fuel-sodden road and the whole lot had gone up in flames.

The hundred or so villagers who had been watching the show took off like rockets. So did I, beating out my flaming arms and legs as I ran. Having successfully put out my own fire I rushed back to the others who were frantically trying to extinguish the Mini. We rolled the car back on its wheels and in a few minutes the fire was out. Damage appeared to be only slight, and the most serious thing was that the throttle cable would not work. It had to be replaced by a length of wire run to the inside of the car, and operated by hand.

Miraculously the engine started and Timo was away. Stuart yelled at the Dunlop boys and myself to give chase in case any other faults developed. Off we went through the dense Saturday afternoon traffic, lights blazing and horns blaring in a desperate attempt to get Timo to the next control on time. After some 15 miles of really hairy motoring the Mini began to slow and eventually stopped. The fire had done more damage than we thought. The engine was cooked and that was that.

All-round service

Of course, not all rally service is as dramatic as that. More often than not it is simply a question of routine, having to be at a certain place at a certain time, remaining there until the rally has passed through, loading all the stuff back into the car and driving on to the next service point. But, as is so often the case, things are seldom as simple as they seem, and the servicing of international rallies is no exception.

Each year our International Competitions Department services on average some 14 major rallies at home and abroad. Basically the aim of the operation is to provide Castrol-using drivers with lubricants, technical assistance and, in fact, any help which our man-on-the-spot is able to give.

Quite often a service car will supplement the service organisation of a factory team and will carry one of the works mechanics plus all the various spare parts, tools and other equipment necessary to service the factory cars. A recent extension to our service arrangements has been the inclusion, on some events, of a vehicle carrying not only oil but a comprehensive tool kit and welding gear plus a host of other useful odds and ends solely to provide repair facilities to private owners.

Rally service crews often have to perform remarkable rebuilding feats under difficult conditions, when the Castrol service crew will be expected to lend a hand. Here, on the 1971 East African Safari, Ford mechanics Ken Wiltshire and Robin Vokins removed the gearbox of Joginder Singh's Escort, repaired the damaged selectors and had the car back in the rally in just under three hours.

Our service personnel have to be jacks-of-all-trades. In addition to being oil men they have to be mechanics and need to be as handy with the spanners as they are with the oil can. They have also to be resourceful and act on their own initiative, even to the point, if necessary, of drastically altering a complicated service plan at the last minute.

Probably one of the most difficult situations involving service-plan changes occurred on the World Cup Rally. Due to weather conditions, the organisers had to make major route alterations in Chile and northern Argentina about 11 hours before the rally was due to restart from Santiago, Chile. The changes involved three Castrol service points which had been set up previously to provide in total some 1,500 gallons of special high-octane petrol as well as about 300 gallons of oil. Two of the service points were in Argentina, where it was impossible to obtain precise information regarding the new route. A phone call to the rally headquarters in Santiago revealed that, although a part of the new route involving two of our service points had been fixed, the decision regarding the remainder would not be made till the following morning. After many midnight phone calls and dragging all sorts of folk out of bed, we managed to make arrangements for two new points on the known section of the modified route. The location of the third point, San Jose de Jackal, was only established the following morning after carrying out an exhaustive recce of the area. After some desperate last-minute panics, everything was set up just minutes before the first car arrived.

Naturally not everything works like clockwork all the time. Some years ago during a continental rally a service crew arrived at a certain village and began to look for the rally control. Having driven round the place for about an hour without success, they asked a local policeman if he knew where the control was. He did but was curious as to why our people wanted to know because, as he informed the astonished Castrol pair, 'the rally came through here yesterday!'

Service fleet

The cardinal sin in the rally-service business is missing a service point, and hence reliable transport is as essential to the service crew as are the wares they carry. Our service cars therefore have to be impeccably maintained and this work we carry out ourselves. Our vehicles are left in virtually standard trim and the only special preparation they receive is confined to fitting stronger rear springs, rally-type lighting equipment, competition brake pads and linings and occasionally wider wheels. Naturally, for events such as the Monte Carlo and Swedish Rallies, we use studded tyres. No demon tweaks are done to the engine for we feel that an increase in horsepower is often accompanied by a decrease in reliability. Spares carried in the cars are kept to a minimum because there just is not room, and these are limited to such items as a plastic windscreen, plugs, contact set, fan belt, gasket set, a selection of bulbs, a coil and possibly a fuel pump.

Even though the cars average more than 30,000 miles a year, breakdowns are remarkably rare. They do happen, however, and it is often the silliest failures that cause the greatest disasters. Once, on an Alpine Rally, one of our cars shed a fan blade. Instead of doing the normal gentlemanly thing and piercing a hole in the bonnet, the errant blade neatly decapitated the distributor. Enquiries revealed that the nearest fan and distributor were in Paris, some 500 miles away. The only solution was to hire a car. The bill was ridiculous, as was that for the spares.

In any given rally our teams may have to provide a lubrication service for as many as a dozen different makes and types of car, ranging from small two-strokes such as the East German Trabants to the two Rolls-Royces which competed in the World Cup Rally. Such a wide variety of cars demands a wide variety of lubricants. To meet these needs our cars often carry as many as six grades of engine oil and an equal assortment of transmission lubricants. Additional items include brake fluids, greases and, in the winter, anti-freeze.

The lot tots up to something over 50 gallons per car, or 5 cwt. Added to this are tools, grease guns, gearbox and rear axle topping-up pumps and a drain-off pump. This last item is basically part of a fire extinguisher which has been adapted to suck oil out of an engine via the dipstick tube and facilitate oil changes when the sump plug is rendered inaccessible by the sump shield. All service cars carry a roof-rack-mounted dural sign which serves the dual purpose of making the vehicle readily identifiable to the rally drivers and providing publicity.

Of necessity our service personnel travel one man to one car and thus servicing a big international event can be physically very demanding. On events such as the Spa-Sofia-Liège it was not unusual to drive 800 miles in a day, as well as 'doing' a couple of service points which might be four or five hours in duration. On most rallies one is fortunate to be able to sleep in a bed one night in three and quite often it is impossible to eat more than once a day. Service points have a diabolical habit of coinciding with meal times! Weather conditions can vary from the −40°F temperatures experienced on the 1966 Swedish Rally to the searing 100°F of the 1969 Acropolis. The roads range from motorways to the dizzy heights of the Col de Restefond in the French Alps. On rallies such as the 1,000 Lakes in Finland you can drive all day and see hardly any tarmac, and in Sweden never have anything but snow and ice under your wheels. In Peru and Bolivia altitudes are such that breathing becomes a problem and changing a wheel can leave you absolutely exhausted.

Planning service

Rallies vary widely in character and pose varying problems in the organisation of service. On events such as the San Remo, Tour de Corse and 1,000 Lakes, which all have pocket handkerchief routes, two service cars can cover the rally efficiently. However, events such as the RAC Rally of Great Britain and the Monte Carlo Rally require a minimum of six vehicles to do the job properly.

When planning service for any event several points have to be borne in mind. Obviously service points should not be too far apart (200 miles is about the maximum desirable) and they should be at places where the competitors will have enough time to make use of the service provided. For that reason we endeavour to place our service cars at the end of long, rather than short, sections whenever possible. Another important consideration is that the service schedule has to be worked out so that our people have ample time to travel from point to point. High-speed thrashes with heavily laden vehicles are discouraged.

Marathon service

No chapter on rally service would be complete without some reference to those motoring extravaganzas, the modern trans-global rallies, pioneered in 1968 by the *Daily Express* with the London-Sydney Marathon and followed in 1970 by the *Daily Mirror* London to Mexico World Cup Rally. One of the greatest problems confronting drivers on these events is that of petrol, for in parts of Asia and South America, not only are there very few petrol stations but the fuel obtainable is often of extremely poor quality.

Because of this, Castrol arranged on the London-Sydney Marathon for special supplies of high-octane fuel to be made available in Iran, Afghanistan, Pakistan and India. In Iran, the National Iranian Oil Company were extremely helpful and guaranteed supplies of 97 octane fuel to the rally drivers at many stations on the route. Furthermore, they readily agreed to our suggestion that payment for the fuel should be effected by a voucher system. The vouchers, each for 20 litres, were printed in Iran, in Arabic, sent to London and distributed by us to competitors before the start.

The quality of the fuel rather than its availability was the major snag in Afghanistan. The locals get most of their petrol from Russia and its octane rating is in the low 80s. The only solution here was to try and obtain permission to import 97 octane fuel from Iran specially for the event. In order to do this I made the trip to Kabul and, after several meetings with government officials, the Afghan authorities very kindly agreed to let us bring in 5,000 gallons of Iranian fuel.

In Pakistan and India, fuel with an octane rating of 90-plus is only obtainable in the larger towns. Through our associate company Burmah-Shell we were able to arrange for supplies of 'the good stuff' to be placed at strategic points along the rally route.

It's almost certainly true to say that the Castrol service operation on the World Cup Rally was the largest single undertaking of its kind in the Company's history. Our brief was to provide a comprehensive lubrication service along the entire route, plus a fuel service in South America for the British Leyland and Ford factory teams. The service was extended to cover certain private owners nominated by British Leyland's Peter Browning and Ford's Stuart Turner.

The European part of the route provided no difficulty and this we covered with nine service points manned by five service cars from England and staff from our branch companies in Germany, Italy and Austria, plus our agents in Portugal. The big headache was South and Central America. As with the Asian section of the London-Sydney event, the main problem was fuel but on a very much larger scale. Whereas we had only to fix up fuel in four countries on the London-Sydney, the South and Central American sections of the World Cup Rally involved no less than 15 countries. Furthermore, instead of the dozen or so fuelling points we had arranged in Asia, we were now going to have to budget for 50. Again we had the problem of quality, as octane ratings varied from as low as 80 in Bolivia to 100 in Mexico.

The British Leyland and Ford rally engineers stated that an octane rating corresponding to British 2-star grade was just about as low as they wanted to go. This we were able to arrange in the countries in which the fuel was poor (Brazil, Bolivia, Ecuador and Costa Rica) by mixing the local brew with an equal quantity of PN 100/130 Avgas. In all the other countries the fuel was of adequate quality and so we used the local stuff. The exception was Argentina, where we were able to get hold of 100 octane racing fuel.

The locations of the service points themselves were fixed on the basis of information fed back to England by the British Leyland and Ford recce crews. Armed with these details I made a whistle-stop tour of South America, visiting 14 countries in 28 days and detailing our service scheme to our various branch companies and agents. I was able to give them precise information on the siting of the service points, their timing and the quantities of oil and fuel required at each one. Also it was necessary to make hotel bookings for the service teams and arrange a travel schedule which would enable the eight people who would come out from England to cover as many of the service points as possible and yet leave sufficient time to take care of unforseeable snags such as cancelled flights, bad weather and delays to the rally itself.

Other points to be ironed out were methods of distributing the fuel and oil to the service points and also the provision of adequate manpower to hand it out. Most of the service points were to be in the middle of nowhere and so trucks had to be hired and rendezvous meticulously worked out. In some cases we were able to hire a petrol station for the day, but that was not possible very often. The labour problem solved itself as a result of the enthusiasm shown by our South American colleagues, who conjured up people as if by magic. In fact, a total of more than 300 people took part and they handled some 25,000 gallons of petrol and more than 3,000 gallons of oil.

Why do we do it? Rallying provides us with considerable technical information which can often be incorporated in new lubricants and also in existing ones. Many of our products first saw the light of day in rally cars. Finally, I suspect that we're all just a little bit mad!

CHAPTER 5

The hot seat

Val Shenton explains what you ought to know about basic navigation for club rallies

NO RALLY CREW is complete without someone in the 'hot-seat', the place reserved exclusively for the navigator. He—or she—needs no special skills, but it helps to have a computer-like brain and a strong constitution, for few jobs call for such versatility of mind and body! The purpose of this article, therefore, is to set out some of the most basic and common forms of club rally navigation, and to give an insight into the preparation needed to make navigation easier as experience grows.

The map

Maps issued by the Ordnance Survey (OS) are the most comprehensive of Great Britain, and for rally purposes those to a scale of 1 inch to 1 mile are the most widely accepted and used. It is essential to become totally familiar with the map and particularly with the symbols at the base of all OS maps. These symbols are often used in route instructions and form the basis for all map reading. Many are self-explanatory and they can be defined into four categories.

The information in the bottom left-hand corner of the map gives the map revision. This is symbolised by a letter and may be accompanied by two further symbols—a line under the letter and/or an asterisk. This shows how up-to-date the map is. Below this is the year of the revision and any minor revisions. This is important because it is usually referred to in the Additional Supplementary Regulations (ASRs) for each rally. The revision required should be born in mind when buying maps, as some dealers do not always stock the most recent revisions. Also, when buying maps it is worth looking carefully to check the accuracy of the printing. It is highly unlikely that an imperfect map will appear for sale, but this is possible. Examine each corner of the symbolised area of the map. If accurate, the corners will have a slightly thicker line marking, with a definite suggestion of one colour having been superimposed upon another. If imperfect, the colour will not appear superimposed on others but to one side of them. Alongside the revision details is a diagram showing the maps in the surrounding area and the amount of overlap, if any.

The next item of information shows the relationship of Magnetic North and True North to Grid North. The lines which run North/South on the map are Grid lines and Magnetic North and True North are shown as angles of deviation from Grid North. This angle varies over a period of years, by a very small amount.

Next follows information showing comparative distances in miles, yards and kilo-metres for measuring; below this is an explanation on reading map references which is dealt with more fully later.

Finally there is a section on the symbols which are used throughout all 1 inch OS maps and which give all the relevant information regarding the area covered. Briefly, these are sub-divided into groups showing road classification, rail classification, waterways, contours, gradients and a series of symbols to identify buildings, landmarks and other relevant information.

The National Grid

A little more at this point should be said about the lines which traverse the OS map. These lines and their numbers relate directly to the National Grid, which is a complex of imaginary lines covering the entire country. The origin of the National Grid is to the South West of Land's End. The lines from this point are repeated at 1,000 metre intervals (ie 1 kilometre) both eastwards and northwards. The Eastings are the lines which run North/South on the map, and the Northings are the lines which run West/East on the map. The squares formed by these lines crossing are kilometre squares.

As the distance across the country, when shown at kilometre intervals, is considerable the numbers along the sides of the map represent only a part of the whole number. These whole numbers are shown in each corner of the map. The line numbers are repeated every 100 kilometres, and to simplify the system further each 100 kilometre square is designated two letters. This is shown clearly on the inside cover of the current folded maps.

Basic equipment for the club rally navigator includes a flexible map reading light, a firm map board, the appropriate 1 inch to the mile Ordnance Survey map, a pencil, a romer for plotting map references and a watch. It's also useful to have a sense of humour and a bottle of travel sickness pills!

The details given in these last two sections form the groundwork for navigation and help the navigator to understand his job more thoroughly. The map, however, is not the only requirement. Here are a few other useful aids.

Basic navigation equipment

In order to plot a route the map needs some support; thick card is adequate, although more sophisticated boards are available. Card, however, forms a firm backing without being too rigid, a point worth knowing before the first emergency stop! You will also need a romer (explained later), kept on a piece of string to hang round the neck, loose enough not to cause constriction, but not so slack as to delay baling out! A stock of pencils is a good investment, to allow for loss or breakage, and they should preferably be soft and black to give a clear line on the map. You also need a soft rubber which will not rub out map markings as well as pencil markings; a good, easy-to-read watch, preferably a pocket watch; and a variety of less useful equipment, none of which is expensive but may make a tricky section of navigation more simple. They are a ruler, compasses, protractor, map measurer (opisometer) and/or dividers, average speed calculator, magnifying glass, clip board for the route card and a few odd pieces of paper, including tracing paper. Ideally they should all be kept together in a strong box, into which spare maps can also be put and which is just big enough to fit into either the door pocket or to keep on the floor or transmission tunnel without being in the way.

Even for daylight rallies it is useful to have an illuminated map magnifier. Certainly for night rallies it is essential to have a general map-reading light, adjustable by rheostat control for brilliance, but which does not distract the driver.

It is also a good idea to spend a little time preparing the map before embarking on an event. Unfolded maps are the cheapest available and have the advantage that they can be folded to your own requirements. You may have to experiment with folding to find a comfortable size which fits the map board and the width available in the car. Avoid, however, folding the map along the kilometre line markings. It is difficult to use the romer on a fold and the line may soon disappear altogether as the map begins to show signs of wear.

It may also help to trim the map by cutting off the white border just outside the black edging. If necessary, mark the map number and the revision clearly in one corner or on the back of the map, and retain any other information given at the base of the map by sticking it on to the map board.

It is also useful sometimes to mark the position where other maps join. There may be an overlap, where part of one map is repeated on another, or the maps may fit edge-to-edge. These marks can be made in the margin, still remaining inside the chequered border, but be careful not to mask kilometre line numbers. (See figure 1).

You may have noticed that a thicker line marks the map in multiples of ten, both vertically and across the map. In order to follow these lines more easily when the map is folded and you are working in the middle of the map it helps to repeat the line numbers, thus making plotting quicker and easier. Select intervals on the map where there is little or no detail, write through the horizontal lines (between the Eastings) and to either side of the vertical lines (between the Northings).

The romer

The romer is a three inch square of plastic or similar material and is a vital aid to any navigator. It provides varying amounts of information according to the make. One of the most popular models is that made by Garford Romers. It gives information for use with $\frac{1}{4}$, 1 and $2\frac{1}{2}$ inch OS maps.

46

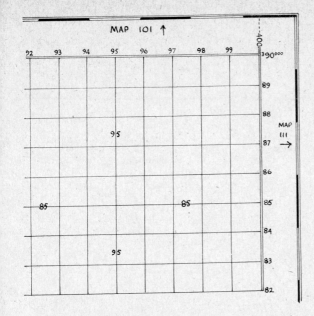

MAP 101 ↑

Figure 1: How to mark up your OS maps with additional information to assist navigation and plotting.

In the case of rallying with 1 inch OS maps one corner is shown as a kilometre square with 100 metre sub-divisions for plotting map references. The romer is also designed to show quick reference measurements of ½, 1 and 3 inches; a sub-division of 1 inch to 1 mile in tenths and 100 yards; an easy to use pencil guide marking of 1 inch to 1 mile in tenths; and formulae for working out average speeds, time and distances. There are also compass markings and a simple protractor with 10 degree interval markings. And that's one heck of a lot of information to cram into 9 square inches!

Map references

Having spoken about the map at some length it should now be possible to plot most forms of navigational exercises, the most important of which are map references. As has already been said, the map is divided into kilometre squares, the lines of which, when traced to the edges of the map, are designated a number. Map references are read by using these numbers and by further sub-dividing the kilometre square to obtain a more accurate point within that square. This can best be explained by the example shown in figure 2.

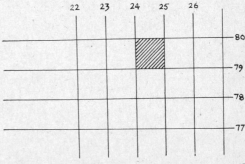

Figure 2: A four figure map reference—the kilometre square.

Four figure references: An example of this would be 2479. Divide the figure into two equal parts, ie 24/79. 24 represents the kilometre line marked along the top and bottom of the map. This is an Easting. 79 represents the kilometre line marked along the sides of the map. This is a Northing. 'Along the corridor and up the stairs' is a popular saying which is a simple aid to remembering which figures to read first. In the diagram the shaded area to the East and North of the point where the lines cross forms the kilometre square 2479. This is a simple four figure reference.

Six figure references: These are a development of the four figure reference and facilitate plotting a more accurate point within the kilometre square. An example is 240790. As in the first sample the figures are divided into two equal parts, 240/790. 24 and 79 are read as before. The third and sixth figures signify 1/10th parts to the East and North of 24 and 79, respectively. In this example the third and sixth figures are both 0, and therefore the point of the map reference is the point at which the two lines 24 and 79 cross.

Reading 1/10th parts within a kilometre square is a little more difficult although they can sometimes be estimated with reasonable accuracy. Rally navigation, however, usually calls for accuracy, especially in densely marked areas where several roads cross. Two methods are possible. A ruler with 1/16th inch markings can be used, 1/16th inch being equal to 1/10th of a kilometre. This involves measuring the required distance to the East and North of the appropriate square, which of course is time-consuming. By far the best method is to use a romer, and for plotting map references one corner only is needed. This corner is divided accurately into a scale 1 kilometre square, and sub-divided into 1/10th parts within the square.

To read a map reference of six figures using the romer follow this simple guide. (See also figure 3.) For example 245795. Divide the group of numbers into two equal parts as before, ie 245/795, and read 24 and 79 as described in the first example. Line the romer up at the point of the marked kilometre square where the two lines cross. Finally, move the romer Eastwards 5/10ths and Northwards 5/10ths. The point of the romer will then indicate a point within the kilometre square accurate to within 100 metres measured on the road.

Eight figure references: These are a further development of four and six figure references to obtain even more accuracy in plotting a precise point. The principle is the same (see figure 4). For example $243\frac{1}{2}797\frac{3}{4}$. Divide the group of numbers as before ie $243\frac{1}{2}/797\frac{3}{4}$ and read 24 and 79 likewise. Line the romer up with the point where the kilometre lines cross. Move the romer Eastwards $3\frac{1}{2}$/10ths (the $\frac{1}{2}$ is estimated) and Northwards $7\frac{3}{4}$/10ths

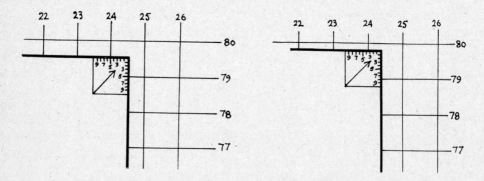

Figure 3 (left): Plotting a six figure map reference with a romer. Figure 4 (right): Plotting an eight figure reference.

(the ¾ is estimated). The point of the romer then indicates the accurate position of the reference given, to within 25 metres on the road.

Another method is to give the fourth and eighth figure (the fractions in the previous example) as a decimal point—the point being omitted. The fourth and eighth figures still need to be estimated but would bring accuracy to within 10 metres on the road. An example is 24357977. The need for such accuracy is questionable, since the width of the road as represented on the map is not to scale.

Directions of approach

Route instructions given solely by map references are often referred to as 'plot and bash'. They may also be accompanied by directions of approach and/or departure. Such directions are normally given as abbreviated compass points and it is therefore necessary to become thoroughly familiar with the points of the compass. It is not unknown for some navigators to draw these on the back of the hand before each rally!

The direction of approach is the direction from which the crew approaches a given point, and the direction of departure is the direction towards which the crew goes from a given point. Such directions may be used to clarify the direction of the route along specific roads, at junctions and to and from controls.

Occasionally compass points may be presented independently of other instructions, for example—Approach the following junctions in order, from the direction given:—SW: SSE: NW: W: WSW, etc.

Instructions by map references with or without directions of approach and/or departure are by far the most popular method of navigation in club rallying. Every navigator should practice plotting them quickly and accurately and finding a route, usually the shortest, from one reference to another. Route cards given by this method are easy to understand and keep to a minimum the time required to plot a route—time being of the utmost importance.

The method of marking the route on the map is a personal matter and best left to individual interpretation. The following suggestions might, however, be helpful. Each point should be clearly marked, by a line across the road at the point of reference, or by a circle if the reference is at a junction. Any approach or departure directions can be inserted by using an arrow and then the route between each reference should be clearly marked, using preferably a soft black pencil which can easily be erased in the event of errors.

The line marking the route should always be kept to one side of the intended route, never on the road marking itself. This makes it easier to read the direction of travel if consistently used, especially when reading down the map or when attention is momentarily distracted from the map. The map should not be turned round so that the navigator always reads up the map. The acrobatics necessary to follow such a habit are likely to render both members of the crew speechless by the end of the event! Marking consistently to one side also makes it easier to see at a glance if turns at junctions are to the right or to the left.

Spot heights

A spot height (SH) is a point which denotes the number of feet the land is above sea level. It is marked by a dot—sometimes hollow—with a figure alongside. In club rally navigation these figures are often used in order to suggest the desired route, or as a 'via' instruction between other methods of navigation, such as map references, for example— Pass through the following spot heights—688, 653, 479 to MR 123456.

Naturally in plotting a route using spot heights the navigator is concerned with those points which are marked on the road, unless otherwise very clearly stated, as opposed to the many others which are situated away from the road. A useful aid when looking for spot heights is a magnifying glass, especially in heavily detailed areas of the map. Care should also be taken to follow the instructions precisely. This is essential with all instructions but there are two very important points to apply when plotting a route using spot heights.

Firstly, the instructions may define that the spot heights should be used in order. Secondly, the instructions may define that only a specific number of spot heights are to be used. These are both sometimes ignored, especially by the less experienced navigator who, as a result, may carelessly drop vital points. Another gruesome navigational method is to direct the route through an unknown number of spot heights whose total height is given. It's all a question of trial and error, using the spot heights in the near vicinity until the correct combination is found. Once more, this is a very time-consuming process unless the right answer is found first time.

The precise siting of a spot height is sometimes confusing when working in detailed areas of the map with similar 'dotty' markings such as parkland or boundaries. Milestones, too, are similarly marked with MS (milestone) or MP (milepost) written alongside. One difference is that spot heights are marked centrally in the road and milestones slightly to one side, a difference easily identified with a magnifying glass—a useful tip when two such markings appear close to a junction, each on a different road.

Tulip cards

Navigation by tulip card instructions is another very popular method derived from the Tulip Rally, which is easy to follow when applied in its simplest form. The tulip card is a series of symbols representing junctions. Each symbol is a diagrammatic representation of the junction on the map. White roads (those that are not coloured on the map!) are not always shown on a tulip card, but when they are a broken line is used in the symbol.

In following tulip instructions it is essential to plot the route on to the map, rather than simply reading the directions to the driver. This makes it easy to correct errors and also allows for further instructions to be applied later.

Illustrated in figure 5 is an example of a typical tulip card showing each junction in turn, which is followed by a brief explanation. The lines of the symbols represent the roads. The circle denotes the point of entry and the arrow-head the destination point. Any lines to either side of the desired route or crossing the route are those roads which are to be ignored.

Figure 5: Examples of tulip type symbols.

In the illustration each junction is numbered. This is the most natural method of presenting the tulip card. The first symbol indicates that the route proceeds straight ahead, leaving a road on the right. The second shows that the route goes right at a 'T' junction; left at crossroads (3); right at the next junction (4); and acute left at a more complex crossroads (5).

Various methods can be used to make a tulip card more difficult. One is to leave out the numbering of the junctions and this could mean that they are to be read in 'any order', a method which calls for the navigator to study closely the symbols to arrive at the desired route. Though numbered and taken in order, certain symbols and their appropriate number may be omitted altogether. They might for instance appear as 1; 3; 4; 6, and so on. The arrow-head or the circle may be left out from some of the symbols. This is not an error on the printer's part! Another trick is to present the tulip card back-to-front or upside down! On some small club events the methods of navigation are so varied as to be unimaginable and often serve only to slow down an event.

Whatever method is used, it is always advisable to look carefully at both the symbols and the map. There should be some resemblance between one and the other and this can often be done most effectively by looking well ahead and by getting a good idea of the overall route. It might even be easier to work the whole thing backwards, starting from the end—assuming the end is known!

When a tulip card is being used over a large area of the map the mileage from one junction to the next may be given, leaving out one or many intermediate junctions. The distances given may be from one junction to the next and/or the cumulative mileage from the start to each junction (see figure 6). This is typical of the road book supplied on most international events, where there is no trick navigation of the type described in this article.

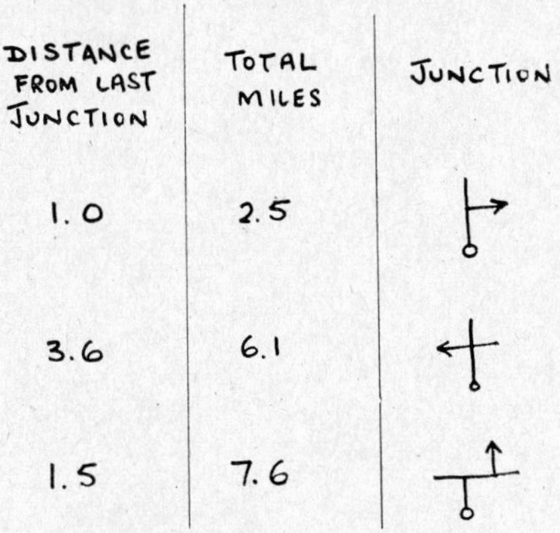

DISTANCE FROM LAST JUNCTION	TOTAL MILES	JUNCTION
1.0	2.5	
3.6	6.1	
1.5	7.6	

Figure 6: A conventional tulip type road book with total and intermediate mileages.

Herringbones

The herringbone bears some resemblance to the tulip card in that it is a series of symbols. Here, however, the symbols are linked into a continuous line (the backbone) with ribs marked to either side indicating the junctions to be ignored. Unfortunately, the shape of the junctions on the herringbone bears no resemblance to the shape of the junctions on the map, as they do on a tulip card, but nevertheless it is essential to transcribe the instructions on to the map in order to show a route. Figure 7 is an example of a herringbone which is followed by an explanation. The junctions are also shown as tulip card symbols in order to illustrate more clearly the possible interpretations of each herringbone junction.

Remember, first and foremost, that the straight line (the backbone) is the intended route. The ribs are the junctions to be ignored. In the diagram the first rib is on the left. This may mean that the route proceeds straight ahead, leaving a junction on the left. But the first junction may not be on the left and all the junctions are indicated. Therefore, this same rib may mean turn right, thus leaving the road ahead on the left (figure 7A). Similarly, the second rib is on the right. Again this may mean proceed straight ahead, or turn left leaving the road ahead on the right (figure 7B). Look at the tulip card equivalents and the reasoning should be clear!

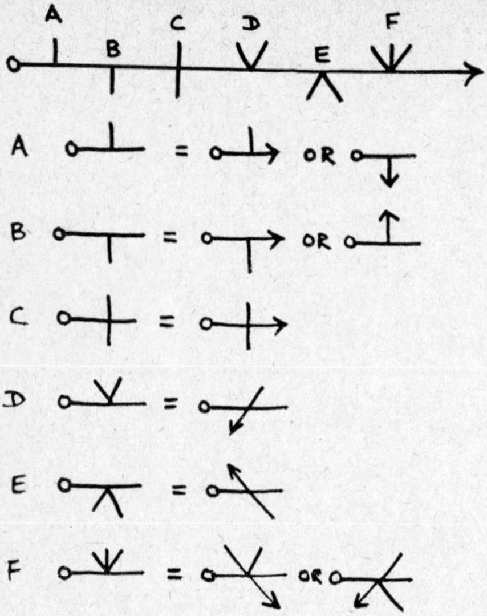

Figure 7: The mysteries of the herringbone instructions interpreted with tulip symbols.

The third ribs are to either side of the backbone at the same point, and mean that the route proceeds straight across a crossroads (see figure 7C). Crossroads are the most obvious and therefore the easiest check in finding the correct route. Even if the route does not carry straight on at a crossroads, the following three junctions in the diagram illustrate the possibilities at a more complex road junction. If two ribs meet from the left it means turn right at the crossroads. If more than two ribs meet from any one side of the backbone it means seek an exit leaving that number of junctions on the side indicated (see figure 7 D, E, F).

Always remember when plotting a herringbone that each and every junction is symbolised. It may be that some junctions are a long way apart, and at other points very close, as at a triangle or staggered crossroads. The distance between the junctions is not readily observed when looking at the herringbone diagram. White roads may or may not be shown, according to the instructions. If they are shown, as on a tulip card, they will be indicated by a broken line.

As with the tulip card there are several variations on the herringbone, though thankfully these are not often encountered. One variation is to join the two ends of the line to form a circle or 'figure 8' shape. The difficulty is that the start and finish may not be shown. The proximity of crossroads is an obvious help, but failing this it is a question of trial and error and can once more be time-consuming. Another complication is not knowing whether to read the circle clockwise or anti-clockwise; it may be shown. Nevertheless the method of reading the herringbone is still the same.

Map references, spot heights, tulip cards and herringbones are possibly the most common methods of navigation found on club rallies. The variations mentioned about tulip cards and herringbones are by no means widely used, but serve to illustrate the many variations possible in most forms of navigational instruction. Whatever form they take, a thorough knowledge and understanding of the OS map is essential, in order to be able to plot a route on the map in the shortest possible time. Although largely common sense, it also helps to become familiar with the many abbreviations that might be used in instructions to keep them short and concise. The following example serves to illustrate this point

—Start, MR (map reference) 468975; .5 (½ mile) turn Rt (right); .2 90 Lt (90 degree left); via SH 545 (spot height 545); SO (straight on) at X rds (crossroads); .6 Rt at T (tee junction) pass under rly (railway) to MR 453925. See how much more lengthy it is to write fully, as the words in brackets show.

Reading the route

Plotting the route, of course, is only half the problem which is placed in the navigator's lap on mounting the 'hot seat'. Equally important is that of reading the route to the driver once it is plotted. The relationship between the driver and navigator is all-important, and possibly accounts for the very few husband and wife partnerships found on a rally!

The crew needs to build up a language of communication between each other. Avoid using confusing clichés, such as the driver replying 'right' (meaning he has understood an instruction), when the navigator's instruction is to turn left. When reading the road it is not necessary to read every bend as it appears on the map, only the acute ones. Experience will show how much information the driver needs from his navigator. There may be a tendency for the driver to slow down more by receiving too much information than would otherwise be the case if driving solely within his own capabilities and vision. He also has to sift out the necessary information relevant to turnings and controls, as well as concentrating on his driving. On the other hand, if the navigator has been reading a fair proportion of the road detail, be sure to tell the driver when he is on his own and you are unable to give assistance whilst plotting. No crew looks experienced when inverted in the ditch!

Give clear, short instructions with relation to junctions and try not to give a string of them all at once. One direction at a time is all that most drivers can consume. Remember the three 'Ds'—direction, description and distance. For example, 'take right at T ½ mile'. The essential information, no more. If the junction ahead is indescribable, tell the driver to slow down or stop as he approaches it and then work it out from there.

Crossroads present no problem when one road is simply directly opposite the other, but try and advise the driver if he is approaching a major or minor road. Staggered crossroads, where the junctions are not directly opposite each other, are best treated as separate junctions. For example, 'take right then immediately take left', instead of 'straight on at staggered crossroads'. The results of adopting the latter method could be disastrous, whereas with the former not only does the driver gather that it is a staggered crossroads but which way the stagger goes.

Road islands are another form of crossroads, though perhaps not frequently encountered. These can be very complicated, as at a motorway intersection. It is best to tell the driver which exit he requires, for instance 'road island, take third exit'. Also give the road number if possible, and watch him round so that the correct exit is selected first time.

As experience grows, and the roads in the more remote areas become familiar, it's possible to build up a fund of information which can be marked on the map for future reference. Some white roads may be rocky, rutted, hard, soft, or worn into gulleys alongside a centre ridge (three-ply). Some may be totally un-negotiable (no-goers), gated, have bad bends, gradients or yumps (where the car is likely to become airborne). Marked on the map for future events, they may help to save valuable time later on and to distinguish you as one of the men as opposed to the boys!

So much of basic navigation is common sense and yet this is frequently not realised until experience grows. No matter how much time is spent on the table plotting, there is no substitute for accepting the challenge and finding out just what it feels like to be a budding John Davenport, who elsewhere in this book gives us an account of the international co-driver's responsibilities.

CHAPTER 6

Marathon musings

Tony Ambrose, organiser of the London-Sydney Marathon and the World Cup Rally to Mexico, ponders on the Marathons

---

THERE IS ONLY one road connecting West Pakistan and India, and even that is not a main road. It is shared by bullock carts, camel trains, pedestrians by the hundred, retired Brigadiers (Indian Army of course—old boy) making their quinquennial pilgrimage to the sites of former campaigns. There's also the odd elephant and a few motor cars. On each side of the frontier is a military zone some 40 or 50 miles wide, which I imagined would be bristling with gun-emplacements, tank traps and grim-faced soldiers to ensure that we did not deviate from the single-track road connecting the two countries. In fact, there was no sign of any military activity and the frontier posts, far from being the grim concrete mini-fortresses which mark their Iron Curtain counterparts, were a series of tents housing the officials responsible for frontier control, immigration, health and police.

The formalities were tedious, for the painstaking methods of the average British civil servant in the lower grades were adopted with relish by both Pakistanis and Indians. If we managed to instil into them the importance of a correctly filled-in form we failed miserably in convincing them that the English language was of major international significance, so the all-important detail of the colour of one's grandmother's eyes is translated into one of maybe a dozen languages and the appropriate hieroglyphics are entered on the buff form.

I first experienced this tedious frontier crossing in February 1968, when it took us nearly three hours to clear both sets of formalities. My mind boggled at the scene which would surely be ten times worse when up to a hundred weary, dirty, irascible rally crews descended upon this frontier post. The cars would certainly be carrying a wide range of spares and equipment, to say nothing of the crews' personal baggage and such puzzling items as teddy bears taken along as mascots. Tempers would become frayed and the London-Sydney Marathon would grind to a halt. My immediate reaction was to neutralise the frontier crossing—that is to say place one official immediately before the first tent on the Pakistan side and another immediately after the last tent on the Indian side and then disregard the time taken to pass between the two officials. In theory this would work, but it was open to abuse by wily competitors who deliberately extended this 'dead' time in order to service their cars without time penalties. The expense of sending two experienced British officials to this remote frontier would be prohibitive. Furthermore, if we were to use this method for one frontier then what about the rest? The point where the only road crosses from Iran into Afghanistan must be one of the world's most remote, and is manned by people who speak not a word of any European language. In fact, a vast team

54

of officials from Yugoslavia eastwards would be required, and the bill for air fares, hire cars and expenses would run into thousands of pounds.

Clearly, to spend money in this manner would not be popular with the management of the *Daily Express*, but equally an event which was not a fair test of skill and endurance would be ridiculed by both national daily and technical press. Negotiations took place in the various countries concerned and through the Embassies and High Commissions in London. Promises were made of 'every possible assistance': some we believed, some were taken with a very big pinch of salt. The result was a compromise and we took a risk on all but two frontiers.

In the event we could have been even more daring, for the co-operation between the Indians and Pakistanis, two nations in theory in a state of war, was superb. The Indians supplied electric current for the Pakistanis, who plied their Indian opposite numbers with food and drink. Competitors cleared both frontiers in 25 seconds, most of which was occupied in shaking the hands of local dignitaries.

Such is the appeal of this type of trans-world event to people who have no particular interest in motoring sport of any form that they are captivated by the thought of two or three chaps, or even girls, climbing into a motor car in London and driving into the rising sun for a month, eventually, whether victor or vanquished, arriving on the opposite side of the world. Even in an era when moon-walking has become a practical if expensive pastime the *Daily Express* London-Sydney Marathon gave adventurous types who regard the motor car as the standard means of transport the opportunity to do something which was competitive. Competitive not only because others were attempting to maintain the same average speed over the same roads at the same time, but also because to do it was an achievement in itself.

When the event was first proposed there were many sceptics who thought that a mere handful of starters would be flagged off and that these would consist either of professionals or of the very rich. Certainly these two categories were to be found in numbers among the entry, but there were those whose bank managers would have slept very uneasily had they known what their clients were about to undertake with only scant funds. Some thought no further ahead than Sydney, and if they had any budget whatsoever for their participation had not bothered to include return air fares or freight for the car. I managed to persuade one or two who intended, after a long weekend in Sydney, to retrace their steps overland in a more leisurely manner, that their cars would be mere heaps of tin if they completed the course. Fortunately, and very generously, the Australian Government agreed to admit all competing cars to Australia duty-free and to permit their sale after the finish. Even so, one young pair of hopefuls, who had set off without even sufficient money to buy petrol for the whole journey and who had borrowed money from fellow competitors in order to complete the trip, sold their Volkswagen in Sydney for less than £100 and then spent the next nine months washing dishes at a large hotel in order to save their return air fares.

This type of enthusiasm distinguishes the Marathon from shorter international rallies, most of which start and finish in the same place. In particular, the Monte Carlo Rally, which has owed much of its glamour in years gone by to the fact that an overland journey in the depth of winter from John O'Groats or Umea to the sunny Mediterranean was quite an adventure before the invention of effective heaters and studded tyres, has now become a doddle in anything but a year of freak weather conditions. The men are sorted from the boys by a race at night over two-and-a-half laps of a mountain road 'circuit' that makes a tangle of knitting wool look like a plumb-line. In short, the difference between a marathon and a rally is similar to the difference between climbing Mount Everest and running up and down a stepladder a million times.

Among the international stars are those who excel in snow or on ice, those who are happiest on smooth dry asphalt with racing tyres rubbing against wheel arches and the 'G' forcing the seat-belt to cut into their shoulders, those others who shine in the deep black slime of wet African cotton-soil or merely the muck and mire of a Welsh farmyard, and even the masochists who long for fog so thick that you can hardly see the end of your own bonnet. If it's ice and snow you're after why look further than the Swedish Rally? For dry asphalt try the Tulip, Alpine or Tour de Corse. The glutinous gluttons gang to East Africa for the Safari and the radar-equipped masochists thrive on the Monte or the RAC Rally. If you are a good all-rounder the Marathon is the event for you.

Starting in late autumn there is a good chance that the European section will include a fair dose of fog. In the mountains of Turkey, Iran and Afghanistan ice or even snow will alternate with dry roads, which are likely to persist until India. In Australia dusty deserts and muddy plains complete the full range of conditions and, if the Snowy Mountains live up to their name, the other varieties can be repeated on the far side of the globe.

Not only does the Marathon call for a crew with a variety of driving techniques but also one which is versatile in its planning and tactics. Petrol supplies vary between extremes. There is, for example, the smartly uniformed Supercortemaggiore attendant on the auto-strada who cleans your screen and lamps before you have had time to sort out whether the several thousand lire which he has muttered is what he wants you to pay for the petrol or his offer for your car. Then there's the one-legged cripple on the edge of Uzbekistan who, in his seventeenth hour of sleep that day, when your car draws up, hobbles on his crutch to a rusty barrel which he somehow manages to tilt so that the evil-smelling brown fluid which he contends is petrol slurps into a leather jug, the precise volume of which was once determined many moons ago by a blind Inspector of Weights and Measures. Equipped with a copious quantity of the said fluid, with which you have filled not only your over-size tanks but every can, bag or bottle which you happen to have with you (because the next similar source of fuel may be several hundred miles distant and the equally sleepy attendant may well have been goaded into even deeper lethargy by a previous competitor), you then find that it takes you 147 miles before you can engage top gear.

By this time you will probably have melted every electrode on your spark plugs and the cylinder-head gasket will be starting to blow. When you get out to fix it you realise why you have been able to average only 51 mph for the past three hours on a dead-straight dry asphalt road. Not only is your car vastly overladen and running on this highly toxic mix-ture of distilled goat's urine and camel dung, but you have been steadily though imper-ceptibly climbing and are now at six-and-a-half thousand feet. When you get out of the car you then realise that, in spite of the fact that the sun has been shining continuously and the heater in the car has kept you comfortably warm, there is a biting wind which chills you to the marrow instantly as it is 12 degrees below freezing.

After the previous six days, in which you have had only a few hours of interrupted sleep, the spanner held by a hand which is sore and numb from gripping the diminutive steering wheel which some fool advised you to fit, slips and takes the skin off four knuckles. Due also to the fact that your diet has consisted of bars of chocolate and cups of coffee, punc-tuated by several frustrating attempts to keep down Asiatic bacon and eggs or its metric equivalent, your temper is not at its best and a job which would have taken you an hour and a half in your own workshop is still not finished after three times that period.

Planning rest periods in advance for the whole of a Marathon is probably a waste of time, but ensuring that each member of the crew gets sufficient rest in each 24 hours is not. Moreover, it must be firmly established among the crew that the resting member or members really try to sleep. It is so tempting to stay awake watching the changing faces of the local tribes or the unusual landscape, but such a course may well lead to mistakes which result in Sydney Harbour Bridge remaining something which you have seen only on a picture postcard.

56

Left: Assisted only by a local enthusiast British official Peter Harper runs a control in South America on the World Cup Rally with little more than a control banner, a table, a watch and his rubber control stamp. Right: The Marathons have brought rallying unprecedented publicity. Australian TV cameraman, Rob McCauley, is caught by the camera of another competing film crew led by Colin Taylor.

Opinions differ, even among the top professionals, as to whether it is an advantage to have a three-man crew on such an event. Before the first London-Sydney Marathon most professionals reckoned a three-man crew to be essential. When he arrived in Sydney, Paddy Hopkirk maintained that he had lost all chance of outright victory because he was weighed down by his third man in a car which was not among the most powerful in the event. To confound this argument the Marathon was won by a three-man crew and at no stage did I hear Andrew Cowan regret the presence of his number three. In fact, when the time came for entries to be made for the *Daily Mirror* World Cup Rally there was once more a three-man crew in the Cowan car, but on this occasion the third man was a Peruvian whose local knowledge and ability to communicate with the natives might have been a great help. Alas, the car crashed before reaching Peru so we will never known whether this advantage would have materialised. What we do know is that in the World Cup Rally two-man crews came through to take the top positions, but it must be remembered that, although it was much tougher than the 1968 London-Sydney Marathon, competitors were given rest halts every two or three days.

I think competitors will still have a difficult decision to make when entering future Marathons. My guess is that if the right two professionals are paired together they must be the most powerful combination, but so often both competition managers and their star drivers come up with some very weird pairings.

It is always tempting to put together two number one drivers on the basis that they will be able to change shifts at a moment's notice should one feel too tired to give of his best in the middle of a critical section. It works in theory, but ignores the fact that neither has been conditioned to sleep while the other is tweaking the car along a ledge at nine-and-a-half tenths, so both quickly become very tired. Perhaps this is not too important if the servicing and refuelling arrangements go according to plan, but when a fuel dump is missing and a quick decision must be made about whether to look for fuel locally or to press on and hope for the best, it is then that the professional co-driver is sorely needed. The combination of the star driver and traditional rally navigator has the obvious weakness if the navigator is one of the 'dry asphalt roads only' brigade of drivers. There are many such 'number twos' in rallying today and the older they become the less likely they are to improve their driving.

It requires a really determined effort by the competition manager and the number one driver to develop the driving ability of a navigator and turn him into a true co-driver. When attempts have been made to find new blood for the number two seat from club rallying, 99 per cent of the candidates have turned out to have so little driving ability that they would never reach a sufficiently high standard or, if they showed any signs of potential at the wheel, it was coupled with a head so big that the bill for the oversize crash-helmet would exceed the first ten years' prize money.

For non-professionals the decision on the number in the crew is probably easier. One of the main factors is the problem of financing the venture and this obviously stands more chance of getting off the ground if the costs can be split three ways. Furthermore, the realistic amateurs banish from their minds all thoughts of outright victory and by so doing channel their efforts towards a sensible goal. Even so, they must be very careful about the

Author Tony Ambrose, nearest the car, checks the Evan Green Triumph 2.5 into the Monza Control on the World Cup Rally. In the striped-sleeve rally jacket is co-driver Hamish Cardno, who contributed the chapter on homologation in this Manual.

amount of insurance in the form of spares, de-ditching equipment, clothing and food with which they burden themselves. It is not very clever if it is the pair of spare rear springs in the boot which causes a rear spring to break! There is no doubt in my mind that most of the cars with three-man crews leave the starting ramp grossly overladen.

Figures quoted for the cost of competing in a Marathon vary enormously and can be as high as £10,000 per entry. This figure may well be true for a works car with full-scale route surveys to be included in the price and a host of very special bits and pieces which are manufactured regardless of cost. When a non-works driver is asked what it costs there is usually a very wide range of figures within which his answer can fall. Moreover, it must be established whether one is talking in terms of gross costs, excluding sponsorship, or whether a net cost. All too often the figure for the wife flying out to spend a few days holiday in Fiji or the Bahamas after the finish is also lumped in. I am quite certain that if a crew is sufficiently clever in obtaining sponsorship the net cost can be kept down to the purchase price of the car and the return air fares for the crew.

When selecting the third crew member it may be more important to assess his sponsorship potential than his driving ability or bank balance. Too many people milk the cow of sponsorship until it is dry. Few realise that the moment that the first cheque, or promise of it, is received from the first sponsor is when the work really starts. If people can see that your sponsors are getting value for money, for instance in the form of press announcements right from the beginning, then you are much more likely to see further cheques rolling in. Be careful not to confuse sponsorship with charity. There are over 20,000 charities registered in England—all of them more deserving than yours. The severely handicapped man who entered for the 1968 Marathon and then complained that the businessmen of his local town had jointly contributed only a few pounds to the venture, ought to have been more concerned with the company that make the valve seals for the hydraulic pump which operates his powered hand controls.

Be generous to your sponsors. If you accept their money it is up to you to tell them how they can obtain the greatest return. Do not be like the young man who obtained sponsorship from a bank for the World Cup Rally on the basis that they were bound to get editorial mention and then omitted to suggest to the bank that they might like to put a decal on the car. He might have got away with it but for the fact that the organisers had obtained sponsorship from a rival bank and each car carried a compulsory decal!

If entries are oversubscribed for a European international rally it is those competitors with the most experience who are allocated the places—probably with a bias in favour of competitors from overseas. If ever a Marathon faces the same problem the decision of the selection committee will be more difficult. So far, both trans-world events have been sponsored by newspapers who were attracted not because they were attaching their names to an event which would happen regardless of their involvement, but by the possibility of creating news, the reporting of which could more readily be done by them than by their rivals. On this basis the maximum encouragement is given to colourful entries and these are not always the most experienced.

Even though there has been room for everyone so far, the organising committee on both events has had a few heart-searchings about entries which, if accepted, might cast doubts on the sense of responsibility of its members. When the Beach Buggy was first nominated for the World Cup Rally, those of us who had any idea of the difficulties to be encountered in the 15,000-mile route could not regard this as a serious entry. We asked ourselves whether these young men had any idea of the temperatures which would be encountered at night crossing a 16,000-feet pass in the Andes. How would anyone get any sleep at all in such a vehicle? Would it therefore crash on the German autobahn when the driver fell asleep and probably involve a non-competing car? How much rallying experience had they between them? None to speak of.

However, further enquiries revealed that these same young men had won a major award in the Round Britain Power Boat Race the previous year by having the courage and audacity to perform very competently in 'Psychadelic Surfer', an inflatable rubber boat! Much to the delight of the newspaper, their entry was accepted and they were an extremely newsworthy crew while they remained in the rally. Beset by mechanical bothers due to an extra fuel tank coming adrift, they eventually retired at Sofia, upsetting no one save the girl-friend of one of the crew who waited in the freezing cold at the Monza control for nearly 24 hours. She was eventually rewarded!

Before the 1968 London-Sydney Marathon the committee spent some considerable time debating whether the entry of Keith Schellenberg in his vintage 8 litre Bentley should be accepted. The worry here was not whether the crew had sufficient experience—this was never doubted—but whether the owner should be allowed to risk such a valuable and unsuitable car. In fact, we turned it down, whereupon Keith wrote to Sir Max Aitken, the Chairman of Beaverbrook Newspapers, and queried the sanity of Sir Max's committee. Keith was insistent that this was his motor car and his money and that anyway he had two other 8 litres even if he wrote off this one, so what was all the fuss about! The committee was overruled and certainly the car created an immense amount of interest until it eventually retired in Eastern Turkey when 'the road collapsed under its immense weight'. This I will never believe as I suspect that the road went right but the Bentley went straight on!

When we were in Perth awaiting the arrival of the cars and crews we learned that the Bentley had arrived at Bombay and was being shipped back to the UK. This shows the immense determination exhibited by this crew as, at the time of their retirement, they were much closer to London than Bombay and only a few hundred miles from Istanbul, from which port the car could easily have been shipped.

There was fierce argument within the selection committee about the acceptance of a Land-Rover entered by the 17/21st Lancers and skippered by Lieutenant (now Captain) Gavin Thompson. The regulations expressly forbade four-wheel drive vehicles, but the intrepid soldiers were quite happy to disconnect the drive to the front wheels. We all knew that the vehicle would be far too slow to stand any chance of success, but should we deny them the chance to have a go? Frankly, I was worried about accusations of cheating which might be made, even if we checked at intervals throughout the route that there was no drive to the front wheels. Let's get this straight, we did not in any way doubt the honesty and integrity of the officers and men who formed the crew from this very fine regiment, but it was more a case of justice being seen to be done. Their entry was finally accepted and again they were good news value.

British Army Units along the route had been briefed to give support and the whole thing took the form of a military exercise. Defence Attachés from our various embassies appeared with cold chicken and words of soothing diplomatic encouragement and, in fact, were able to afford to these military gentlemen, along with all the other service crews, some small advantages which were not available to mere civilians. Nobody complained. I felt very sorry for Gavin Thompson when they arrived at Kabul late—about 15 hours late —as he had a raging toothache and the hard suspension of the Land-Rover must have given them an uncomfortable ride. Another hour was lost while a dentist was found, on a Sunday morning, to deal with the offending tooth. During these proceedings the Corporal and the Trooper who were accompanying the two lieutenants had one or two terse comments to make about 'the endurement of pain in battle by flamin' orfficers'. Nevertheless, morale was high and the crew aquitted itself well. It was Gavin Thompson who later persuaded HRH Prince Michael of Kent to compete with him in the World Cup Rally— this time in an Austin Maxi. Unfortunately, on this occasion a driving error in Brazil caused severe damage to the front end of the Maxi and put them out of the rally.

Wild pre-start destruction testing for the London-Sydney Marathon paid dividends for Andrew Cowan who pulled off a well-calculated victory with his Hillman Hunter.

Before the 1968 London-Sydney Marathon perhaps the committee was obsessed with the possibility of someone cheating. Certainly, Stuart Turner and I were well aware that the dividing line between rallymanship and cheating is a very fine one and with the biggest prize fund ever offered for a rally the more ruthless competitors might be tempted to take advantage of any tiny loophole left by the organisers. Such a possibility is an organiser's nightmare, for not only might the result be unfair, but the end of the event, instead of being a glorious spectacle, might well develop into a sordid squabble. Both Stuart and I had been deeply involved in the arguments at the end of the 1965 Monte Carlo Rally, when the Minis were disqualified for having the wrong headlights. This dispute, and the uncertainty of who had won, ruined that Monte, detracted from the status of the event in future years and brought the sport of rallying a degree of ridicule.

We were determined to avoid this and for this reason the restrictions on the technical specification of the cars were kept to a minimum. Even the insistence that four-wheel drive vehicles should not be admitted emanated from the Society of Motor Manufacturers and Traders and was not the wish of the committee. Body/chassis and engine block were marked so that they could not be changed, but everything else was free. However, one of our fears was that on the long section from Teheran to Kabul (about 1,350 miles) some enterprising competition manager would charter a freighter and fly his cars or, more feasibly, fly his crews and put in substitutes for this long tiring stage at a critical point in the rally. It was not only to record the feared delays at the frontier that we sent Peter Riley and Peter Cooper to either side of the Iranian/Afghan border. If on future trans-world events a similar possibility exists then it is important that the organisers involve themselves in a similar exercise, regardless of the expense.

The regulation which caused us the most trouble was that defining eligibility for the Private Entrants' Award. While it is clearly desirable to establish a category for the under-privileged it is debatable whether this should be done on the basis of the limited experience of the crew, the amount of assistance received from the motor manufacturer, the fact that the car is owned by a member of the crew, or by limiting the amount of financial assistance available. Apart from the first of these, the others are open to fiddles. The lessons learned on the London-Sydney Marathon, when Michael Taylor's eligibility was in doubt until after the rally had finished, were only partly applied to the World Cup Rally. Here great pains were taken to ensure that eligibility had been established before the start with sufficient time for other competitors to protest, but it was still felt that some of the accept-ances for this category were not in the spirit of the regulations even if they conformed with the letter. The five Citroens were indubitably owned by members of the crews, but they appeared with full works support and, as far as their rivals were concerned, they were suspect as private entries. Only one car, that of Patrick Vanson, survived the journey to Mexico City and he won the Private Entrants' Award.

This improvement in the regulations was one of the ways in which the *Daily Mirror* World Cup Rally was able to benefit from the 1968 London-Sydney. For the professional competitors it was in many ways an improvement. The combination of air charter and freighter for the cars between Lisbon and Rio was deemed to be preferable to the cruise liner which carried both crews and cars from Bombay to Fremantle. This is probably because a professional rally driver like Paddy Hopkirk has itchy feet and feels that he could be more usefully employed doing a further route survey.

Many of the desirable facets of the World Cup Rally were embodied regardless of cost. The continuous severity of the route in South America meant that controls had to remain open in many cases for as long as 15 hours. The fact that there were frequent rest halts in the capital cities through which the rally passed involved the organisers in 'in' and 'out' controls on opposite sides of the city and in manning a rally headquarters in the centre during the interval. The establishment of *parcs fermés* in these cities, with the added complication of a regulation which permitted members of the crew to work on the car under supervision, further increased the need for skilled rally officials. Some 30 enthusiasts were employed and, although all gave their time freely, air travel and expenses for each amounted to almost £1,000.

A good drama relies on the third act for its climax. On the Marathon the last 18 hours contained four very competitive sections, and the top half-dozen competitors were all within striking distance of the lead. Consequently there was tension and drama in plenty throughout the last night and morning. On the World Cup Rally Hannu Mikkola and Gunnar Palm had such a commanding lead in their Ford Escort at Cali, four days before the finish, that the one remaining critical section could hardly be expected to affect the result. In fact, they drove it at touring speed.

Will there be any similar events in future years? I don't know. Certainly there has been talk of Paris-Peking, of London-Tokyo, of Mexico-Munich and a Pan African Marathon is planned for 1973. Military activities in the Far East and the closed frontiers of the Far Eastern Communist states suggest that the first two could come to a grinding halt for political reasons. Similarly, the African states are unpredictable in whom they welcome. The problem of creating a dramatic climax in Bavaria would only be solved if the organi-sers could get round the Federal German laws which have effectively prevented competitive rallying in Germany for some time now.

Whatever the outcome, Tommy Sopwith and Jocelyn Stevens, who thought of the idea of the first London-Sydney Marathon, and Sir Max Aitken, who signed the cheque, created an epic which will find its place in the history books of motoring sport.

CHAPTER 7

Let's get organised

Richard Harper, experienced organiser and co-driver, gives his
views on rally organisation

THE AIM of this article is to discuss the organisation of the club rally, from Closed to Club
to National British level. The object is to get at the bare bones of the event and to find out
what it is that makes one rally more successful than its contemporaries. Pure organisational precision alone, whilst being a very essential part of any sporting event, does not
necessarily ensure that it is remembered. It is the combination of slick and skilful organisation and the creation of 'flair' that I would like to amplify.

Whilst the gigantic Marathon events, like the London-Sydney or the more recent
London-Mexico Rally, have the built-in grandeur and panache of vast distances, and
imaginative organisers are able to make the best use of romantic territory (and occasionally get away with organisational murder), the British event, with a very limited time
schedule and amateur organisation, must clearly be much more precise and definitive.

I feel quite strongly that the requirements of organisation that apply to a National rally
should also apply, with only minor exceptions, right down to Closed to Club level. By
that I mean that the 'team' should in all cases have the same aim and should consequently
be set up in a very similar way and with pretty well the same duties.

I know that there are many excellent events, whose organisers need no encouragement
or advice from me, but I'm sure that everyone who has ever done a rally will have come
across the highly enthusiastic group of organisers who have worked hard for over half the
year and, because they were not set up properly, have only just managed to struggle
through and bring a halting rally to an unsure conclusion. The effort is there but it has
been wasted.

Objective

Always aim to have a rally that is clean, slick and without any time-wasting elements.
Always see that you are fair to the car, driver and navigator. There is nothing smart in
confusing a crew with vague or clever instructions that you've had months to work out.
The only result of this is to upset both the crew and the resident whose garden they turn
round in!

Your object must always be a result that is fair and won in genuine competition. If this
is achieved you have happy crews, sponsors, residents and hoteliers, all of whom will be
pleased for you to come back again next year. You will also receive a good press and
publicity which can only be good for the Club.

Method

To establish a set routine and pattern for the event right at the start is, I believe, the most important single goal for any organiser. This means that not only must the team be established early but so must the individual duties of each member of that team. This may seem obvious but it is no use having someone agree to be a Sector Marshal if he doesn't know what this entails and eventually finds that he hasn't got the time to do the job properly. If he has to be replaced it is better that it should happen at the initial meeting rather than a week before the rally. It is never safe to assume that old so-and-so will do some creative job for you if you don't detail it to him early and make sure that he understands and accepts all the implications.

So, having put the rally into the hands of the Clerk of the Course, give him the whole responsibility and, apart from progress reports to the Club Committee, let him have his head. The Clerk of the Course, who should generally also operate as Chairman of the Organising Committee, should start to establish his team. Having accepted the job he will already have these people in mind so I would recommend the following procedure.

Call an introductory meeting about eight months before the scheduled date of the rally, at which the following will be provisionally fixed and minuted by the Secretary of the Meeting: (1) Ratify the position of the Clerk of the Course who will run the whole event. (2) Appoint the Secretary of the Meeting who will be responsible through the Clerk of the Course for all correspondence and legislative requirements, of calling meetings and keeping the minutes. (3) Appoint the Chief Marshal who will be responsible for the overall marshalling picture and for the complete PR coverage of the route. (4) Appoint Sector Marshals to do the physical PR work and the actual running of a short sector of the route (say about 25 miles and covering some six to eight controls). (5) Appoint the Entries Secretary, if the Secretary of the Meeting feels that he is being overworked! (6) Appoint a Results Captain whose responsibilities are obvious. It is a good idea to have him in from the start but he can be appointed afterwards if necessary.

This basic team will be the Organising Committee who, through the Clerk of the Course, will bring the rally to its conclusion. Having discussed at this meeting each individual duty, and had it minuted, an agenda should be made for a regular monthly meeting at which each of these officials will make a report. This may seem unnecessary, but if you insist that this happens even where there is nothing to report, and this fact is also minuted, then the likelihood of even the smaller details being forgotten is much reduced.

Having established the team and its duties one then gets down to the proposed style of the event. The bald facts—date, duration and status—have many significant facets that should not be overlooked, but very often are, which will have an effective bearing on the eventual character of the rally and which may well be discussed at this first meeting. If your detailed organisation is going to be so slick it is nice to build character into the rally too.

Date

The date chosen for the event can to some extent affect the likely weather conditions. Clearly, there is the difference between summer dryness and winter snow and fog. The event that is rendered very tight and difficult by ice or fog on the night would be nothing like as interesting on a moonlit spring evening. And there are more subtle things to look for. There are many rally roads used in winter time for their difficult, twisty features that are perhaps even tighter in the late summer and autumn months as a result of overgrown foliage and hedgerows. I would even say that many areas that are not truly competitive during winter months because of the flatness of their terrain, and which are consequently rejected by searching organisers, become extremely interesting and difficult to drive on when the already narrow roads are much reduced in width and vision is consequently reduced by the lushness of the hedges and verges in summer and autumn.

Facilities

It has been said that once the start, fuel halt and finish are established the major route problems have been solved. That is not quite true, but it is certainly no good leaving these points till last. You may think it obvious, but so many events have fallen into disorder simply because of lack of attention to these very points. In all three cases you must make sure of sufficient space, facilities, comfort, accessibility and time for people to complete whatever task you impose on them at that point. The number of competing crews expected will have a bearing here but it is also as well to remember the status of the event and of the competitor, and the impression that you want them to take away with them.

At your start area, for instance—is there room, and time, for every car to be scrutinised effectively according to your regulations? If you are issuing route details here, is there space for all your competitors to plot the route comfortably? If your Chief Marshal is assembling his marshals here, is there room for them too, both for parking and at the fuel pumps? Have you visited all the local residents within earshot to explain the unexpected noise and bustle?

All these points apply to whatever fuel halts you arrange and, at the finish, you must clearly make sure that adequate facilities exist. There must also be arrangements made for your results people to work effectively. If it can be assumed that your documentation and marshalling has been good, your results people should be able to produce detailed placings on this type of event very soon after the last competitors' scheduled finishing time. The question of results is discussed later, but it must be clearly understood that quick and accurate results depend more on accurate and well thought-out documentation and positive marshalling on the route than just the arrival of an army of willing mathematicians at the final control. This is one good reason for the inclusion of the Results Captain in your original team.

Groundwork

Having established your team and regular meetings, each official sets about his task. The Secretary of the Meeting makes a schedule of the appropriate dates on or before which he must contact the various authorities (ie RAC, MOT, National Parks, Farmers Unions, Councils, landowners, garages, etc). The Chief Marshal, with his Sector Marshals, starts rounding-up support and recording their various marshalling experience and skill since these always vary so much. The Clerk of the Course thinks in terms of the best use of the territory chosen, and the timing and results systems to be used. Everyone's ideas are discussed at the regular meeting. (It is a useful point that very often potential officials can be helpfully trained at these meetings, just by sitting in and observing.)

Route

Your prime intention will be to concentrate as much competitive motoring into the distance and hours that you have available. Your second priority must be to see that the route you lay out is completely honest to all competitors. Since less-experienced crews will inevitably form the larger part of your entry, it would be stupid and inconsiderate to relate your route and time schedule to the seeded entry at the front of the line. Always bear in mind that you are wasting rally time and competitors' time if large chunks of your route prove to be too easy. On the other hand, there is little point in pushing ahead so hard, either by too tight a time schedule or by the use of consistently rough going, that everyone becomes heartily sick of the event before it is half-way through. That is the surest way of reducing next year's entry, and a compromise must be found.

In my experience a route and schedule that gradually tightens over each batch of five or six controls has the most testing effect. In other words, the schedule should result in the quickest crew losing a penalty minute at each fifth or sixth control, not due to a sudden tight or rough section, but as the result of a steady build-up of lost seconds at each control until the inevitable whole minute appears. This naturally requires a good deal of careful thought in planning exactly where the controls will be placed. However, even in comparatively easy territory, it is generally possible to embrace competitive sections into batches of five or six, even if it means bringing in very easy linking sections of road to join one batch to another.

Placing of controls becomes important for two main reasons. Firstly, it is evident that studious selection of control sites can alone tighten any road section. Careful thought and imposed pressure from the maximum use of every junction and feature of the landscape not only provides the most interesting competition, both for the driver and for the navigator, but also goes three parts of the way to producing those lost seconds. The second reason for close attention to this point is that careful planning can very positively reduce the number of marshals required for any given stretch of route, without reducing in any way its competitiveness or its penalty potential. The accompanying illustrations of a hypothetical piece of rally route, show what is meant.

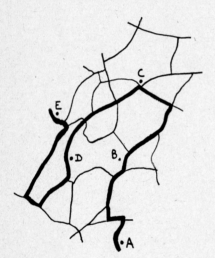

Figure A

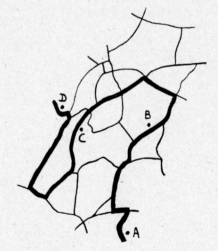

Figure B

In illustration A you have the conventional set-up of five controls covering four shortish sections and about eight miles of route. This is wasteful planning for one of two reasons. Either by re-siting the controls, as in illustration B, you reduce your marshals from five to four for the same section of road or, far better, increase the mileage from eight to 12, using more competitive territory to much greater advantage at no extra cost to your marshalling strength. This brings in more testing road reading for the navigator and more effort from the driver, as in illustration C. I am quite sure that, of the three sections here, C would be by far the most enjoyable to drive and certainly the one on which an organiser could guarantee to penalise the vast majority of his entry. Remember that A uses just as much of your map, uses just the same number of marshals and needs just as much PR coverage to produce only two-thirds as much route of much less competitive rallying.

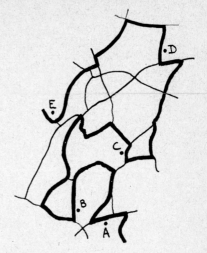

Figures A and B (left) and C (right) illustrate a hypothetical rally route traced from an Ordnance Survey map, showing how to use the local road network to the best advantage.

Figure C

The only addition that one might make to this type of routing is the inclusion of a tie-deciding section. Known these days as selectives, and timed to the second, they provide an interesting departure and enable the use of the odd two or three miles of more testing territory. I would never recommend lavish use of these sections on anything less than a Championship event, and particularly not where there is a shortage of marshals capable of accurately timing up to 100 or so cars to the second. Your results party will have enough problems without trying to interpret cockeyed time cards!

Documentation

Having settled your style of route you must then get down to the very important documentation of the rally. Whether the paperwork is lavishly printed or simply duplicated, the object is always the same. Keep it as simple, clear and concise as possible. The RAC lay down a pattern for the Additional Supplementary Regulations for an event which must compulsorily be published by the promoting club. This is covered, together with MOT requirements and permit application procedure, in RAC Standing Regulations. However, the remaining competitors' paperwork and documentation is left largely to the Clerk of the Course. These, in turn, probably comprise: (a) additional supplementary regulations; (b) final instructions and entry lists; (c) route card or roadbook; (d) time-cards; (e) additional bulletins or amendments; and (f) final results.

Bring in your Secretary of the Meeting on the compilation of a, b, and f, your Chief Marshal on b (in relation to the start and fuel halts), d and e, and your Results Captain on d, e and f.

Timing

Whatever timing system you propose to use, the one rule must be 'make it absolutely simple'. The less the marshal has to write and record, on the fewest pieces of paper, the more accurate he is likely to be. For this reason I would always recommend a variation of the 'card system' (ie a system whereby the marshal issues a separate card at each control to each competitor, bearing the competitor's time in minutes only). This results in the competitor eventually producing a pile of cards, one for each control he has visited, whenever and wherever you want to collect them.

The card system, whilst a little more expensive than others, has two great advantages. It allows the marshal to work much more quickly and accurately than if he were required to record times on a competitor's roadbook. Simply, he can sit quietly recording times in the same place on each one of his pile of cards before the competing car stops at his control. As the competitor arrives he is handed a completed time card clearly and accurately endorsed. This is so much better than the marshal chasing about trying to endorse a roadbook that is generally presented upside down and back to front, and which he promptly slaps on to the wet and muddy roof of the car in search of a surface upon which to write! After 20 controls the poor Results Captain is then expected to produce an accurate result from the pulp!

The second advantage is one of clarity for, apart from the difficulties already mentioned, the marshal is, in his rush, frequently inclined to endorse a roadbook in the wrong place for his particular control, especially where the competitor has missed the preceding two or three controls. It is sometimes impossible to be absolutely sure where such an endorsed time should properly appear and to which control it refers. Penalty assessment then becomes guesswork.

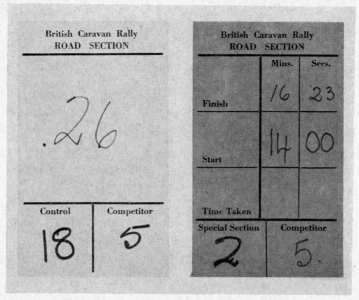

Time cards. Figure D1 (left) and D2 (right).

Route and time cards

Illustrated is a sample of a route card showing all the information necessary to clearly define a route. There is no surplus information, but it is being as helpful as possible (see figure E). The time cards (see D above) show all that is needed to require the minimum of endorsement from the marshal. In the case of the ordinary time control card (D1) all the marshal needs to write is the whole minute at which the competitor reports. To write hours and/or seconds is quite superfluous. Minutes are all that are taken to complete the section so minutes are all that he should be interested in. In the case of the other

CASTROL RALLY MANUAL

ROUTE BOOK

Times shown in Heavy Type are Standard times of Departure and should be adhered to, to avoid penalty, except at Special Section Start Controls, where no road penalty will be applied. Bear in mind however that **All Time Controls** are subject to road penalty.

A Miles to Next Main Control and Petrol	**B** Visit in the Order Given	**C** Direction of Approach	**D** Standard Time (Car 'O')	**E** Scheduled Time =Col. D+ comp. no.
120	**MAIN CONTROL 1 START** SHREWSBURY SMITHFIELD 118/512 157 Depart to N.W. Standard Time of Departure		**21.30**	
	via 118/490 169	S.E.		
	via 440 178	N.E.		
	via 434 141	N.N.E.		
	then A458 (T) to			
80	**S. SECTION 1** Afon Gam Start - - 117/013½ 076 Finish - - 932 005 Time Allowed 14 mins.	N.N.E. N.W.	**23.00**	

Figure E, showing a typical route card.

two places on this card, the 'Control' spot would be filled in prior to the start and the 'Competitor' space by the competitor himself. All you then need to do is to ensure that the cards are collected quickly (to prevent any swapping taking place) and passed to the results team.

For the Special Section time card (D2), which covers incidentally both the start and finish controls of that section and which is timed to the nearest second, the start marshal marks full minutes and seconds on the appropriate space, allowing sufficient time for the competitor to be given a count down start on that recorded minute. The competitor then hands the card to the marshal at the finish control to have full minutes and seconds recorded. The results team make the subtraction when this card is handed to them together with all the others. The whole endeavour by the marshal must be speed, accuracy and clarity and as they do not all have the same experience and skill it is vital that their duties are simplified. It is a very useful cross check, incidentally, to have him keep a record of what he has recorded by means of a simple, pre-worked check sheet. The competitor's number and the time at which he reported are recorded as a check should any dispute arise later.

Results

There are many methods of working out results. The one aim is always to preset your system so that everything possible is done beforehand. Slow results must be the absolute irritant, while instant results sheets always create good feeling and comments.

A few tips might be mentioned here. Give your competitors an envelope, suitably prepared for each of the sections where you intend to collect the time cards. Have a marshal cross check with the competitor the number of cards presented, and have them placed in correct order to assist the results team. Have your first batch of results envelopes ferried to the results team as early as possible, say from the halfway halt, so that they can start to get on with the job. Remember that the first hour for a results party is always the slowest, when they are all getting their first, practical sight of the job. Let them get this hour over in the relatively undisturbed period before competitors start to arrive. Always keep the party isolated and bar competitors from the office. Queries should be made to a separate marshal, for reference to the Results Captain.

Chief Marshal

To go back to the pre-rally organisation, there is one very important man, the Chief Marshal, whose work should be entirely completed before the day of the event. I would lay down his responsibilities as follows, and remember that his work should be reported and minuted at all of the rally meetings.

He will allocate to his Sector Marshals say 25 miles of rally apiece. Their task is two-fold and it is by no means 'gilding the lily' to have so many people involved. They will complete the whole PR exercise for their sector and, because they spend all their time in that relatively small area they will have an intimate knowledge of it. They will know all the residents, gate owners, policemen, road works, diversions and no doubt publicans! Through the eventual marshals' meeting they will also know all the marshalling crews working on their sector and have a much closer working knowledge of their patch than if the Chief Marshal attempted the whole thing on his own. PR coverage also becomes a much easier task which, with a bit of luck, might be accomplished in a single day. Multiply one Sector Marshal's actions and effort all the way around the rally route and you should have a neat and tidy package.

The second important duty of the Chief Marshal is the organisation and arrangement of the marshals' meeting. He, and the Clerk of the Course, will need to see that the Sector Marshals, who by this time will have completed their PR duties and sorted out likely problem spots, in conclave with their particular Control Marshals, and go over the exact job of each one of them so that no mistakes are made. Samples of the time cards and control clocks must be available to be seen. Pay particular attention to those marshals who are to man the most important controls. Going back to my original illustrations, how unfortunate and unnecessary for the 12-mile section (figure C) to be wasted because you have failed to get through to your marshal at Control E and he has failed to understand what his exact job entails. All you get out of that is a wasted 12 miles of good rally route!

Public Relations

This is a much abused phrase these days but it is an absolute and compulsory duty of any Clerk of the Course to see that a 100 per cent effective coverage is made of the whole of any rally route. This means a visit to the door of every single resident on the way. There is no substitute for this and no attempt should be made to short cut this prime duty. This is another good reason for having your 25 mile Sector Marshal!

I have found that a personal chat is good but a short, written outline of the event, detailing times and dates, is very effective. I used a PR letter in Wales for several years which, printed in both Welsh and English, was slightly 'doctored' in the Welsh translation to produce a version that was always highly amusing to the proud Welsh reader on his doorstep, whether farmer, housewife or Minister of the Chapel. The inevitable result was that, whilst most were initially dour and set against the passage of the rally, a reading of our idiot attempts at Welsh made friends of us all and rallying was happily accepted!

CHAPTER 8

Flat over brow . . .

John Davenport, rally contributor to Autosport and works Lancia co-driver, explains the mysteries of pace notes

NOT TOO LONG AGO, when I started club rallying, marked maps were in their infancy and only a handful of navigators had a set of maps with all the inaccuracies corrected and the hidden dangers added. Marked maps today are standard equipment, though some are better than others, but the 'professional amateur' on British club rallies distinguishes himself now by using pace notes over mountain passes like Tregaron to Abergweysn. Back in the 1950s, that particular road was largely unsurfaced and few people could say with any certainty just where it was. Still, pace notes were then but a recent addition to the international scene.

It is very difficult to establish with any certainty the first occasion that pace notes were used for, like so many things, they evolved gradually. The most publicised use of a pace note system came when Stirling Moss won the Mille Miglia in 1955 with Denis Jenkinson as co-driver. On that occasion 'Jenks' read the information off a long roll of paper on which they had transcribed all the details of the course that had been noted down while they drove round in practice. This was not strictly a rally application and, with the demise of the Mille Miglia shortly afterwards, it was left to rallymen to pick on the idea and develop it for their own use.

Perhaps the team which should take most credit for modern pace notes was the old BMC crew under Marcus Chambers. For many years, John Gott used to prepare for them route notes and assessments and it was a natural development for these to grow more detailed on the difficult pieces of road. It only needed a spark of enthusiasm from Tony Ambrose and pace notes were soon the order of the day in the BMC team for all their crews. A good idea spreads fast; other British crews started using them and at one time John Sprinzel and Willy Cave used to prepare complete pace note sets for the Monte Carlo Rally, which Castrol used to print and hand out to drivers running on their products. It might be a bit presumptuous to say that pace notes spread from the British crews to the rest of Europe, but certainly this is true to some extent and helps to explain why British co-drivers have been so successful in international rallies and continue to be in great demand by foreign teams.

What are pace notes?

It is simplest to say that pace notes are something which the co-driver of a rally car reads back to the driver in order to tell him the severity of each bend on the road *before* he reaches it. This covers everything from making notes where bends are identified by

Without pace notes or local knowledge the driver above would have no idea of the severity of the corner ahead. It could be a fast open bend allowing him to maintain his rapid approach speed, alternatively it could be a dangerous hairpin like the one shown below. Perhaps the gap in the wall was made by someone who did not have notes!

mileage, right up to the most sophisticated notes where even lines through bends are noted. Nearly all pace notes are written down in a form of shorthand, but it is as well to point out now that, in just the same way that two drivers may have different ways of describing the same bend, two co-drivers may have different systems of shorthand. Naturally most of my explanation will be based on the system that I use, but this is not to say that it is the best and indeed continual evolution is a good thing.

The system which you use may be cribbed wholesale from another crew or you may create your own or you may do a little bit of both, but it must be a combined effort on the part of the driver and co-driver. It is no good the co-driver insisting on calling a 90 degree bend a 'grotty left' if the driver is going to get confused. The important thing is to try the system in practice and, if there is anything which is misleading or difficult to distinguish, decide on a better alternative between the two of you and change to it.

Most systems grade the bends into about eight to ten categories, ranging between a flat-out corner and a hairpin. This figure seems to be the optimum, as in the heat of the moment a driver would have difficulty in differentiating between say 20 or 30 grades of corner. For the same reason it is best to stick to words or expressions which have some real meaning, which is in itself a description of the speed of the corner. You can use whatever words you like to describe corners in a pace note system, like 'ping right' or 'pong left' to describe quick and slow corners respectively, provided that the driver understands the code. This is all very well, but even the greatest master spies have forgotten their codes at times and they were under considerably less pressure than a rally driver on a stage. Hence it is much better to stick to expressions like 'flat' and 'slow', which are not only short and concise but have a real meaning unlikely to be forgotten by the driver when under stress.

A lot of French rally drivers use a system which is based on the co-driver reading out the speed at which the driver has previously assessed that he can get the car round the corner. I suppose that if you have done a very high-speed recce in a car exactly similar to the rally car, this can be a good system. However, I feel it has two drawbacks which should be avoided if possible. The first is that the notes are very subjective in that they try to describe the corner by saying how fast a particular car and driver can get round it. They say nothing of the weather at the time, so that in fog or snow your approach speeds may be seriously affected by lack of visibility or traction. On the other hand, if the factory has found another 20 bhp for your rally car you may find yourself constantly with too high an approach speed. Finally, the numbers involved are going to complicate matters in that not only are they longer to say (measured in syllables) but they are going to get confused with the distances between the corners. If you chant out 'fifty' how is the driver to know if you are talking about yards or mph?

This brings us to the consideration of distance in pace notes. At one time it was thought enough merely to record the bends and their severity, but gradually more and more information on the distances between the bends, and how they are linked together, was included. At the present stage of pace notes I would say that this information is equally as important as the severity of the bend itself, for accurate distances—or 'links' as I prefer to call them—make the notes easier to read and enable the driver to have greater confidence that the notes are tying up with the road. It also greatly increases the value of notes in fog, dust and other bad visibility conditions. Links start with big distances like 100 yards and come down in whatever increments you feel suitable—most divide that into four lots of 25 yards—until you get bends that have no proper distance between them or which follow immediately on top of one another.

Pace note systems

I shall now explain my system so that you can see some practical examples. Perhaps I should say that the basis for this system is what I was taught by Vic Elford in 1966 and

FLAT OVER BROW . . .

BURZET 4.

SL 100 KR + FL 50

SL · R + KL + SR ·

LKR SL SR · LSL 100

KL FKR + FL into KR + FL SR 50

KL + R + LFL tightens into LFKR opens +

+ SL 50 R · SL 50

FKL + SL 70 LSL 100

[JUNCTION] △ L/c 150 TURN KR 50

SL + LSR tightens 150 C 100

SL SR 70 LFKR + L 200

A typical page of pace notes—part of the Burzet special test on the Monte Carlo Rally. Note that each page has the name of the test and the page number written at the top. The wide margins are left for later amendments and allow a good hand grip without obscuring the information.

that additions and modifications have come with the help of Ove Andersson and Simo Lampinen. As you will see in the illustration on the facing page, we have nine classifications of severity, here illustrated as right-hand bends. If you were to count the left-handers as a separate classification there would be 18!

The whole thing revolves around two bends: one is the 90 degree and is called simply 'left' or 'right' with no prefix and the other is a 60 degree bend which is called a 'K' for no better reason than that it is short, unlikely to be confused with anything else and has the verbal association of 'K for care'. Incidentally, the severity should always precede the direction of the bend as it is the most important of the two bits of information for normally a driver can see which way the road is going! For bends sharper than 90 degrees, we use 'hairpin' and 'open hairpin' for the two obvious ones and 'bad' for a bend more severe than 90 degrees but not in the classical shape. For any of these three that have some special peculiarity there are additional prefixes such as 'tight' or 'narrow'.

The fastest bend in the list is naturally 'flat' and this is usually reserved for such bends that one can be sure will be just that, no matter at what speed you arrive at them. A 'slight' is a bend which is virtually 'flat' and probably won't require a gear change even if you are in top gear. In other words, it is a 'care flat' but we use 'slight' because of the clear meaning that word itself possesses. A 'fast' is a bend that will need a bit of slowing if you

CASTROL RALLY MANUAL

°R	= FLAT RIGHT		LFKL	= LONG FAST K LEFT
SR	= SLIGHT RIGHT		VLSR	= VERY LONG SLOW RIGHT
FR	= FAST RIGHT		+	= AND
FKR	= FAST K RIGHT		•	= STRAIGHT
KR	= K RIGHT		50	= FIFTY
R	= RIGHT		70	= SEVENTY
BR	= BAD RIGHT		100	= ONE HUNDRED
OHPR	= OPEN HAIRPIN RIGHT		FL/C	= FAST LEFT OVER CREST
HPR	= HAIRPIN RIGHT			

John Davenport's pace note symbols translated into the instructions that would be spoken to his driver. The Burzet notes on the left-hand page would therefore be read as follows: slight right, one hundred, K right and fast left, fifty, slight right, straight, right junction and K left and slight right, straight, long K right, slight left, slight right, straight, long slight left, one hundred, etc.

come upon it at high speed, and a 'fast K' is that difficult category of quick corners that are slow and slow corners that are quick.

Next come the 'links', which start quite normally at the head of the scale with '100' and any suitable multiples, but I would advise you to measure anything bigger than '300' with a trip as you would be surprised how far out you can be in judging them by eye. If you get them accurate they can be surprisingly useful in falling snow or fog. Below the basic 100 yards, we use '70' instead of the logical 75 as it is shorter to say and for the same reason we use that funny dot for 'straight' which is the equivalent of 25 yards. The plus sign means 'and' and is used when one bend follows naturally into another with no room for braking or accelerating between. When two bends are immediate we just read them without any link to make it clear that one is on top of the other. The use of the word 'into' is quite widespread but we only use it where a long bend turns into a sharper one.

Finally, we have the fancy dressings such as 'long' and 'very long', and here it is unfortunate that 'long' and 'left' have the same abbreviation. If you are not very precise in writing down the notes, a 'long left' followed by a 'fast right' may read as a 'left' followed by a 'long fast right' but practice helps to avoid this. Perhaps the most important additional note is 'crest' and you will see from the list that we have cribbed the improper fraction notation from mathematics for writing 'over crest'. In rallies like the 1000 Lakes, where notation for crests is very important, both you and the driver soon come to see the

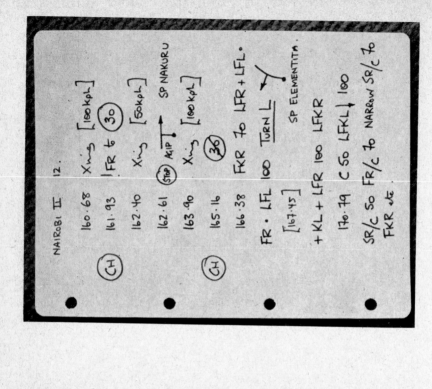

Another page of Safari notes, this time with less pace notes showing how the pace note shorthand can be used for individual bends as well as for sequences.

A page of notes for the East African Safari where the pace notes are mixed in with route instructions, intermediate times, indications of rough patches and changes of surface.

difference between 'fast right, crest, fifty', 'fast right at crest, fifty', 'fast right over crest, fifty', 'crest, fast right, fifty' and 'crest, fifty, fast right, fifty'.

So that is our system for what it is worth. There are things I would like to change, such as the use of the word 'slight' which is so close to 'right', but in practice this has not proved a big problem. The next thing is to consider how to use them, and while I have already said something about this, I want to make one rule about assessment of severity which is most important in practice. Remember that what you are describing is the geometrical severity of the bend which will remain constant whatever the weather or whatever car you are driving. To my mind, there is little future in calling a hairpin right 'flat right' just because it follows a hairpin left. It is much better if you note down the bends for what they actually are and then the driver can drive according to the conditions and the car. It is only fair to point out that there is a strong body of opinion which leans towards subjective notes and there is no reason why I should be any more right than they are; as I said before, you must find a system which is acceptable to driver and co-driver, and all the theories in the world can be wrong when you come to dealing with an individual crew.

Making notes

When a driver is fully familiar with the system the crew is about to use, the quickest way to make pace notes is to drive over the road with the driver calling out the notes and the co-driver writing them down. This may be modified if the co-driver is introducing the system to the driver, and in this case it may be beneficial to use a tape recorder. Gone are the days when the only equipment required in this business was a sharp pencil and plenty of paper, for tape recorder systems of varying degrees of complexity are to some extent replacing the pen and exercise book. To my knowledge, one man has tried doing without any form of written notes at all and that was Carl Orrenius on the Swedish Rally a few years ago. He recorded all his notes on tape and then had a speed-up-slow-down control fitted to the tape recorder motor which the co-driver used to match the speed of the tape to the progress of the car along the road. I regret to say that it was not a great success as it was very difficult for the co-driver to achieve perfect synchronisation.

At the moment, tape recorders are used to reduce the time it takes to do a reconnaissance and give the advantage that the notes are written up in the relative comfort of a hotel room instead of inside the car. They can thus be neater and will probably not require re-copying before the rally. The big drawback of taped notes is that, as yet, you cannot have simultaneous replay and the possibility of correcting as you drive over the road for the second time. It means that the co-driver has to copy out the notes from the tape on to paper and there is seldom any useful work that the driver can do during that period. Thus for events like the Monte Carlo Rally, where you may spend a whole day going over one test, it is still better to use traditional methods and write the notes—however roughly—the first time. You can then correct them as you want on subsequent runs over the test. At their present state of development, tape recorders only come into their own on a rally like the Safari, where you are making 'once-over' notes for hundreds of miles.

One thing to bear in mind when writing notes is the sort of notebook you are going to use. Universally acclaimed as the best are those ruled spiral-bound notebooks (with the spiral on the left) which you can get almost anywhere, for with these it is possible to remove the spiral, change the order of the pages and then re-bind it with the same spiral. Very rarely do you get a chance to recce a rally exactly in the order in which you will do the tests on the event and, in any case, it is more convenient when re-copying notes to be able to do them in the order that suits you and then put them into the correct order for the rally. You may also be using notes from the previous year's event combined with some new notes, and this enables you to bind them up in the right order for this year's event so that you don't start reading Chartreuse notes over the Col de Perty!

FLAT OVER BROW . . .

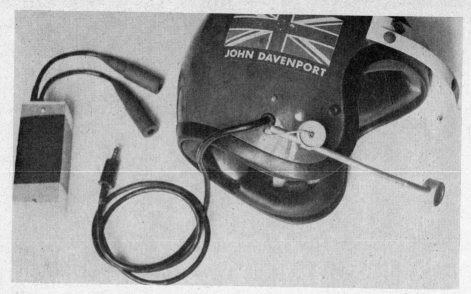

An intercom set is essential for reading pace notes with the unholy row that goes on within a rally car at speed on rough roads. The one above is typical, with a noise-cancelling microphone mounted on a light alloy boom and a simple jack plug connection to the amplifier. With this system no switch is required, for the action of plugging in the connections switches the amplifier on. When pace notes are needed but crash helmets are not (on long-distance events such as Marathons and the Safari) the lightweight headphone set (below) is used.

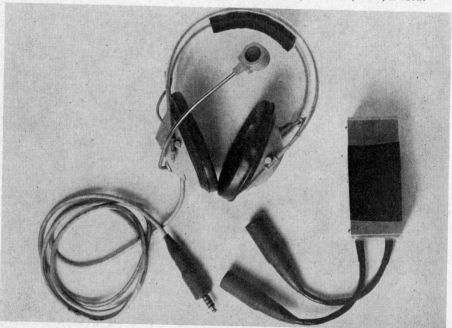

Incidentally, I find that a ball-point pen is the best thing for actually writing in a car, though whenever I copy notes I do it with a black Pentel type on to white paper so that, if I have them photocopied, I get the best reproduction. Also the firm black outlines that you get with this type of pen are much easier to read when they are jiggling around under a map light in a car. I try never to put too many notes on a line and leave considerable margins so that I can hold the notes in both hands and use my thumbs to indicate the line being read. This means that you are not likely to lose the place even if the driver causes the car to jump, spin or even roll. I used to cross off with a pencil each note as I read it out but I find that experience has now rendered this unnecessary.

When to use notes

In just the same way that the preparation of the car—whether by a works team or by a private owner—is the responsibility of the driver, pace notes are primarily the co-driver's province and he will make most decisions concerning them. This starts right at the beginning of the recce when it is his job to put the route on to a map and then, either using his previous knowledge of the event or just by expert guesswork, decide where pace notes will be needed and which is the most economic way of visiting all the tests and tight road sections so that the notes can be done. Sometimes just a look at the map, even on a rally with which you may be totally unfamiliar, is enough to tell you what is going to be difficult enough to require notes. On the other hand, you may see during the recce that one section always has fog on it at midnight, which is the time you will have to drive it on the rally but—since you cannot make notes in fog—you must recce in daylight, when of course the section is easy.

As in so many things, it is experience that counts plus a nice pessimistic streak about what is possible to drive in time. Perhaps this is one reason why British co-drivers have been so successful as partners to the Finns and Swedes, as their training ground of British navigational events has given them a deep-rooted suspicion of organisers and sections that look as though they will be on in the time allowed. Add to this the fact that the English language is suitably monosyllabic to give a clarity and brevity of expression in pace notes unrivalled by any other European language and you can understand why young Finnish drivers, whose talents might get them into a works team, usually have to wait a year while they master English!

Having said that the co-driver is the one to choose where notes shall be made and used, I must add that he should bend to the driver's wishes if the driver wants to use notes in a place where they are not 100 per cent necessary. The co-driver's responsibility is to make sure that there is no difficult or impossible section where they do not have notes at all. He also has to concern himself with the business of getting them copied or written out before the rally starts, and here again planning plus the driver's co-operation are needed. On some events, the note-copying may take days and it is no good if the driver keeps the co-driver out right up to the start of the rally, buzzing over the tests and making final corrections on the rough copy of the notes, if they are not going to be in any state of readiness by the time of the rally. Finally, the co-driver should concern himself with the equipment used to relay the notes to the driver during the rally.

Intercoms

Most teams in international rallying today use an intercom, for gone is the time when you rallied in comfortable quiet cars, and the widespread use of glass fibre panels, open carburettor throats and 'efficient' exhaust systems has made communicating with the driver very difficult. As with the notes themselves, tastes differ but the Mach system from Sweden, and Lustraphone and Rho Videotechnik from England all have their adherents and are very good. The latter two use a microphone fitted to a boom on the side of the helmet, while Mach use a microphone tucked away in a chin strap fitted to the helmet strap. The most important things are that the system should be foolproof and strong while at the same time giving good reproduction and excluding as much outside noise as possible.

The Rho system does this by using sound cancelling microphones which seem to give very good results. I used this system on the 1971 Monte Carlo Rally and when we broke the exhaust manifold the only way we could talk to one another was to wear the crash helmets and intercoms all the time. Whatever you select it has to be comfortable, which means choosing a proper helmet to start with and, since it has to accept two ear-pieces, it is better to pick one that is a shade too large rather than one that is a very snug fit.

The latest developments in the intercom field include the use of free-standing headsets with boom microphones for use on long rallies, where it would be tiring to wear a crash helmet all the time but it would also be equally tiring to have to shout above the car noises for 36 hours or so. These plug into the same amplifier as the crash helmet intercoms so that it is possible to use both on the same event if this proves to be convenient.

Reading the notes

There is a great deal for a crew to learn about the use of notes, especially concerning just how they should be read over to the driver. Naturally the notes have to be read out *before* you get to the bend or the hazard concerned, but just how much before depends on many things. If one is going downhill through a series of quick bends it may be necessary to read some two or three bends ahead for the driver to anticipate properly the sharper bend further on down the road. Going uphill through a series of hairpins, hardly any anticipation at all is required as the car is moving comparatively slowly. Then there is the question of reading the distance immediately after the bend if it is a fast one or waiting and reading the distance separately if it is a slow one. So many of these things will depend on experience that I can give you only the barest indications that such considerations exist, and then say that the individual crew must develop its own criteria for reading the notes.

Finally I want to say something general in connection with pace notes. I remember that when I did the Castrol notes with Gunnar Palm and Bill Barnett for the London-Sydney Marathon we discussed whether to incorporate pace notes in them, but finally we didn't because of the vast distances involved and the relatively low average speeds required. On the World Cup Rally, however, many people made much wider use of pace notes as they enable the driver to keep up a better average speed without caning the car to death, as well as enabling the co-driver to pin-point with great accuracy bumps or pot-holes which would be difficult to find if you had just taken a mileage to them from the start of the section.

Pace notes can be started at a particular mileage in a section and thus incorporated in the middle of a Tulip-type roadbook but, as with special stages, it is much better to try and fix some landmark for the place at which your notes start. In choosing landmarks, one has to be very certain that they will not be moved. Ove Andersson and I left the road on the 1967 Polish Rally when a road sign that we were using to pin-point a bend had been washed away by heavy rain! I don't suggest that you personally check all landmarks for their permanence, but it is better, let us say, to choose a house rather than a road-mender's shed for such a purpose. For much the same reasons, always mark each page with the name of the test plus a number so that it can be identified if a sudden draught blows all your notes on to the floor just when you are re-binding them, as once happened to me.

With all these cautionary tales, the whole business probably sounds terrifying to the layman, whereas it is really very straightforward. Most co-drivers look upon pace notes as a godsend, as they give them something to read while the driver is doing his best to terrify them and impress the spectators. Which reminds me of one last thing. Always have a pen or pencil in your hand while reading notes on a stage because, if you crash, it is as well to mark the place for the driver will doubtless wish to put in a correction and it is better to do it while his memory is fresh!

CHAPTER 9

The Motoring News/Castrol Rally Championship

Geraint Phillips—'Verglas' of Motoring News—relates the background to a popular championship intended for amateurs, but open to all

---

IT IS SAID that the sport of rallying owes its origins to a band of enthusiasts who had become a little bored with the artificiality of circuit racing, and even a trifle blasé about point-to-point races from A to B. They needed something more from the object of their enthusiasm, the automobile; something tough and strenuous which taxed both mind and body and yet was capable of stimulating their sense of humour.

Rallying was thus born. But it was indeed a versatile brainchild, and in the years which followed it underwent a detail metamorphosis which—though it kept the original concept —transformed it into the fast, virile and popular sport which it is today.

At its highest echelons there is a fringe of hard-bitten professionalism, though even the few who go rallying for their bread and butter haven't forgotten the fact that it is still a sport and still a great provider of tremendous fun. Between these and the mass of enthusiastic amateurs there is a layer, slightly wider than the professional one, of in-betweens. These are enthusiasts whose basic urge—other than those classified by Freud—is to go rallying for the pleasure it gives them but whose ability, as persuasive talkers as well as drivers or navigators, is such that they are sponsored in some way or another in return for whatever publicity the sponsor is able to extract for his outlay.

Having mentioned those strange people called navigators, whose skills are talked about elsewhere in this book, and having at least mentioned that there are amateurs and professionals in the sport, I have routed myself to the subject of this chapter, a championship intended for amateurs but open to all-comers.

Unlike athletics or boxing, where the fence dividing the amateur and the professional is so well defined that each class is kept almost pathologically sterile from infection by the other, there are no separate events, nor series of events, for those who go rallying for fun and those who do it for payment. Bare-chested professionalism is allowed to fight it out with modestly vested amateurism in the same ring. It is perfectly natural that the professional should be better at the game than his amateur cousin. He has to be, or he wouldn't remain a professional for very long. It is equally natural, therefore, that all the big plums, the top international awards and the championship laurels, are plucked by professionals.

When competing at international level, amateurs are usually content with the satisfaction of the competition. Obviously they do their best, but in such events as the Monte, the Thousand Lakes or the RAC Rally of Great Britain it is quite apparent from the outset that, barring wholesale retirement, it is the paid works driver who is going to win. At the other end of the scale, there are plenty of small rallies all over Britain to keep the amateur enthusiast happy; rallies which are unsullied by the attentions of factory teams. On these, the enthusiast can avail himself of a night brimful of sporting entertainment, knowing full well that he has the same chance as anyone else of going home with a piece of silverware to mark the achievement.

A decade ago, there were events in the middle bracket; those which didn't really attract factory cars but which claimed the attentions of the country's best amateurs so regularly that competition, although always friendly, was invariably as fierce as on any top-flight international.

In the lower scale, clubs and associations of clubs had their championship series. At the top the works teams could find all they looked for in the European Championship, later to be sub-divided into series for both drivers and manufacturers, and extended beyond Europe insofar as manufacturers were concerned. The contented amateur, rallying his Mini on Saturdays, taking it to the seaside on Sundays and to work on Mondays, had plenty to choose from, and the works teams, just beginning to develop their publicity awareness, had an ample international calendar from which to choose.

But what of the men in the middle? What of the British competitor who was prepared to travel from Perth to Plymouth in search of the most severe, hard-won rallies available outside the FIA list? There were plenty of high-quality events to occupy his time, but at the end of the year what did he have to show for a string of victories or near-victories which put him in a category higher than most? Furthermore, what of the under-rated, oft-forgotten chappie called a navigator who sat alongside the wheel-twirler all night, putting his life in his hands, telling him where and how to go and generally acting nursemaid for the budding primadonna? In club events he was recognised. Even in club championship series his skills were not unrewarded. But in international championships he was a mere also-ran. He got his share of the loot; he even got into the presentation photographs, but at the end of the year when the championship awards were being dished out he became no more than a helper who had already been amply rewarded throughout the year by the free lifts around the world. Happily, this is not the view of the professional competitors themselves, but the various championship regulations are still in need of pretty drastic revision.

But whatever you may think of the administration of upper-crust and bottom-rung championships, the one in the middle was the worst of the lot. The British National Rally Championship, administered by the RAC, recognised only the skills of drivers. Navigators were completely ignored. It was quite unthinkable that in Britain, where the finest carto-graphic skills in the world were centred, the ability of men capable of transforming a map into a radar screen should go unrewarded. What was needed was a national championship divided into two categories, one for drivers and one for navigators.

In 1960, Motoring News, which was then fast developing into the newspaper which catered for the needs of Britain's rallying community, decided to do something about it. Informal discussions were held at after-rally breakfasts and eventually the paper published the announcement that it would itself, quite independently of any other organisation, run a championship which would recognise navigating ability as well as that of a driver.

The selection of rallies which would make up the championship series was something which needed careful attention, and here the likes and dislikes of the competitors themselves (for whom the series was being created, after all) were taken very much into account. There was no wish to cut across the series forming the RAC Championship. Indeed, when a list of some 20 prospective qualifying events was drawn up there was a marked lack of similarity between the two groups.

The RAC Championship was, and still is, based on events which are of national status at least. In theory, that is the basis on which any national championship should be formed.

Reigning Motoring News/Castrol Rally Champions, driver Jimmy Bullough (left), a Company Director from Lancashire who also won the Championship in 1967, and Don Barrow, a mechanical engineer from Cheshire, who has won the Navigator's Championship four times in its ten-year history.

In practice, it's not always such a good idea. The mere acquisition of national status does not guarantee an event's quality, and there were many restricted events which were much tougher, and more popular, than some of the nationals. Hence the dissimilarity between the two series which has persisted right through the past decade.

When it first appeared in 1961, the Motoring News Rally Championship was indeed well received. Within a very short time it became the goal of British rally enthusiasts. Competition became fiercer and, to cater for the demand, qualifying rallies became tougher. Quite a number of the RAC's qualifiers also appeared in the Motoring News series, but it was the latter championship which created the greatest interest and which was followed with greatest enthusiasm. Soon it became the case that crews set out to tackle the MN series and at the end of the year the winning driver found that he had also picked up the RAC trophy on the way. This was not at all good for the RAC Championship which, after all, was the official national series. The situation has so far remained unchanged, but the voice of dissention became louder in 1971 and there are hopeful signs that a change may be imminent.

Rallying, like everything else, is far from exempt from the erosion of time, and it is hardly surprising that the passing of a decade should have left its mark on the sport. Rallying has changed enormously since the championship began, which is not such a bad thing, really, for what sensible sportsman would deny his sport its natural development? The biggest change came in the mid-'sixties with the creation of ministerial legislation to control motorised sport on public roads. We still had the RAC's General Competition Regulations, of course, but now we had the bobbies to keep their eyes on us as well as the men from Belgrave Square. It turned out that the coming of the Motor Vehicles (Competitions and Trials) Regulations was really a disguised blessing, for they served to weed out the inefficient organisers, leaving the sensible ones to get on with the now-complicated job of running worth while rallies.

One effect of the new regulations was the creation of extra administrative work for organisers. In an effort to ease their burdens, there was a sudden urge to run rallies which centred all the competitive motoring on special stages off the public road. For a while, forest rallies were the rage, and many of them appeared in the championship, but the cost

83

The drivers who have come up through the ranks of club rallying and whose consistently fine performances must in time bring them a works drive. Above: Chris Sclater with Martin Holmes on the 1971 Circuit of Ireland when they finished 2nd overall. Below: Will Sparrow, the 1970 RAC Rally Champion, with Nigel Raeburn on the 1971 Fram/Castrol Welsh Rally in which they finished 2nd overall.

Qualifying events—1972

Date	Rally	Organising Club
January 29	RED DRAGON RALLY	Port Talbot MC
February 19	RALLYE BRISTOWE	Tavern MC
March 4	RALLYE DUBONNET	Sporting Owner DC
March 18	CYTAX RALLY	High Moor MC
April 15	NUTCRACKER RALLY	Aberdare MC
August 12	PEAK REVS RALLY	Ludlow Castle MC
August 19	GREMLIN RALLY	Brecon MC
September 2	STOCKTONIAN RALLY	Stockton and District MC
September 9	CILWENDEG RALLY	Teifi Valley MC
September 23	AGBO RALLY	Owen Organisation MC
September 30	PLAINS RALLY	Knutsford and District MC
October 7	ILLUMINATIONS RALLY	Morecombe CC
October 14	TOUR OF MULL	2300 Club
October 28	TORBAY RALLY	Torbay MC
November 4	SHENSTONE RALLY	Shenstone MC

of running such events escalated when the Forestry Commission began charging organising clubs for the use of forest roads. Many excellent special stage events are still held each year, those which have survived being run by clubs affluent enough to stand the cost.

Forest rallying is immensely satisfying and popular, not only among British competitors but also among our fellow sportsmen overseas. One need only ask in Scandinavia what they think of the RAC Rally to discover the world-wide respect for British forest roads, the engineers who created them and the officials who run rallies on them. But as far as the Motoring News Championship was concerned, there was some doubt as to the wisdom of having special stage events as qualifiers. The championship recognised the skills of navigators, but was it fair that Fred should collect more points than Joe simply because he'd been chauffered quicker along the forest roads? After a few years of trials, special stage events were cut out for that reason.

But special stage events, particularly those on forest roads, were not only popular but vital to the progress of the British rally driver, particularly if he wanted to compete with any chance at all in international events. Scandinavians can drive on loose roads whenever they wish; our own opportunities for such practice are limited, and it is cause for celebration that forest rallies have not disappeared from the calendar. Perish the thought that they should ever do so.

Just as the need for a worth while championship was felt some ten years ago, there is a real need now for a drivers' championship (not navigators') based on special stage events. The RAC Championship seems tailor-made for it, and it would take very little adjustment to make it fit the bill exactly. Already many forest events are included in the series, and it would benefit the sport immensely if this were to become an off-road series, leaving the driver/navigator combinations to continue their enjoyment of the Motoring News Championship. Already there are signs that this may happen in the not-too-distant future.

One of the features of the MN series over the ten years since its inception has been the sort of chain reaction which it has created. Rally people are pretty discerning folk, and it is very unlikely that they will return a second time to an event which has been a failure, ie a rally which is poorly organised or run over a dismal route which isn't nearly as testing as it could be. This point is always watched when the time comes to select events for the next year's series, and it has come to be regarded that an event which is chosen for the championship will undoubtedly represent good value. Consequently, there is always a heavy demand for places on such events, and it is the rule, not the exception, nowadays for championship qualifiers to be heavily over-subscribed within a very short time of their regulations being published.

It takes very little intelligence to realise, therefore, that the way to a full field (usually numbering 120 cars) for one's event is to have it in the championship. The only way this can be achieved is by ensuring that it is of the highest possible quality, and we have the situation whereby there is as much rivalry among organisers to set up the best rallies as there is among competitors to win them. The result is a steady and healthy upsurge of good quality rallying, even among events which are not in the championship, the weak and inefficient falling by the wayside.

When the championship started, it was based on some 20 events. Popular opinion was that this was too many, so it was gradually whittled down to 15. The 1971 series was intended to have 15 qualifiers, but a cancellation dropped the total to 14, each contestant's nine best scores to be taken into account at the end of the year. It is one of the principles of the championship's administrators not to interfere with organising clubs in the running of their events. Very broad outlines are given, and it is entirely the province of organisers to choose their own style. This way, there is no fear of any popular rally losing the character by which it has come to be recognised over the years. Another point is the absence of any need to register at the start of a year as a championship contender. It is felt that anyone who is good enough to get into the first ten in any of the qualifying rounds deserves to be allocated the appropriate number of points, whether he has filled in some kind of form or not.

It would be quite inappropriate to write about the MN Championship without mentioning a company which has given its support to all forms of mechanised sport for more years than most of us would care to remember, and has actively aided many an individual rally—as well as teams and drivers—to fulfilment. That company is Castrol Limited. In 1969, Castrol offered its support to the championship, the intention being to help the organising clubs, and the competitors, as much as possible. The overall prize money was doubled, but only to bring it up to a total of £450 divided among ten people. To make the championship too lucrative would attract the professionals, and it was not the wish of anyone concerned to put the series completely out of reach of the ordinary clubman with meagre resources at his disposal. Various organisational aids were also offered to the clubs concerned, and it wasn't long before another automotive company, the Lighting Division of Philips Electrical Limited, also came along with a collection of worth while awards—but still keeping the whole concept of the championship within the amateur bracket.

Where does the championship fit in on the ladder to stardom? That is a question which has been oft asked in rallying circles. Success in the series is no sure-fire way to a works drive, as many have discovered, although most Britishers who have eventually joined factory teams started as rank amateurs and progressed to, and beyond, events such as those which make up the series. But it's the 'beyond' bit which counts, and anyone with his sights set on a manufacturer's contract should eventually aim at international events and as much experience as possible outside Britain.

Whatever their ambitions, or lack of them, competitors taking part in the qualifying rounds of the Motoring News/Castrol Rally Championship will nevertheless be assured of keen, healthy rivalry in one of the most friendly atmospheres of present-day competitive motoring. Whatever a few frowning, humourless characters have to say about the 'serious business of rallying', the thing to remember is that it is still a sport and should always be treated as such.

CHAPTER 10

Rallying in the '70s

Stuart Turner, former Competitions Manager of BMC, and now Ford of Europe's Director of Motor Sports, tries to forecast the future

SOME 20 years ago, an Autosport editorial forecast that rallying had perhaps two years to run before being hounded out of existence by public opinion. It is still just as difficult to make an accurate guess at where our sport is going. The big question mark is over the future of extravaganzas like the London-Sydney Marathon and World Cup Rally, because these create so much interest that they bring rallying to a wide general public, instead of them being things taking place in the still of the night just for *aficionados*.

We badly need them to continue but they started as something of a British gimmick and if they are to develop further then more continental manufacturers must be coaxed into entering—and perhaps we should look to continental sponsors to run them. Nothing says you *have* to have newspaper backing to run a Marathon; it could even be argued that press and television coverage would be greater if one was backed by, say, a cigarette company.

The next World Cup football competition takes place in Germany, so there could be a 1974 Mexico-to-Munich Rally, then in 1978 the football saga is staged in South America so then there could be a Munich-Buenos Aires event, thus keeping the World Cup event going into the 'eighties. It then needs a London-to-Sydney or Paris-to-Peking slotting in between the World Cup events for there to be a major event every two years (which is the maximum that rallying can stand). I then see us moving into the 'eighties with a round-the-world rally, although don't ask me how it would be run or where the route would go— let Tony Ambrose sort that one out!

Will the cost of these events become too great for them to survive? The organising teams are still learning and there is no doubt that a future World Cup Rally could be run for half the cost of the last one. If running to a lean budget means slightly fewer controls than the purists would like, then that is the price we have to pay for having such rallies at all.

Air transport between continents could play a vital part, not only in reducing the number of days competitors need to be away but also in maintaining public interest. Market research after the London-Sydney showed a high percentage of people under the impression that Ford had won; this was because Roger Clark led on the long run down to Bombay, while the relatively short sprint across Australia didn't leave enough time to rebuild interest after the tedious boat crossing.

Political stability around the world could affect long-distance events, although perhaps not quite as much as might be feared. India and Pakistan patched up a quarrel raging before the London-Sydney long enough to guarantee swift frontier crossings, and Latin

American countries fighting over football even offered to move their battle zone to get the World Cup Rally through. So it can be argued that rallying has a real part to play in international understanding.

I said earlier that we should be looking for continental sponsors, but we must bear in mind that these long-distance events will always appeal most to the strange sense of adventure present in the British, which means that a majority of entries will come from the UK. Therefore, a Mexico-to-Munich World Cup Rally should perhaps land at Liverpool and incorporate stages run down through England to Dover, then the continent. Sponsors need domestic exposure to justify their support.

It is argued that Marathon events drain money from conventional rallies. This is partly true perhaps, but is more than compensated for by the fact that they bring in new sponsors, some of whom stay on to support other events. This influx is vital at a time when so many events are ailing.

The Monte Carlo Rally seems likely to go on for ever, although no longer heavily supported from the UK. A drive to Monte is within everyone's reach nowadays, which has perhaps taken some of the winter glamour out of the rally but, to replace this, it is fought over such magnificent special stages, in the full glare of European publicity, that it now has as high a reputation as it ever had. Monte Carlo nowadays needs to fight hard for holidaymakers' money against the greater attractions of less moribund resorts and the rally /and, of course, the Grand Prix) are so vital to the Principality that it is difficult to see it letting the rally die.

A question mark must be put against rallies in Sweden and Finland, although for different reasons. In Sweden all motoring sport faces opposition from a vocal body which has perhaps over-reacted to one bad accident. It seems almost unthinkable that a country which produces such fine rally drivers should ever think of banning the sport, but remember that they have managed to ban boxing over there. We can only hope that, if nothing else, their own car industry emphasises that it needs the rub-off from a strong home sport to help its exports.

Finland has a different problem, namely too much public interest. This leads to so many crowds on the stages that the police have difficulty in controlling them. However, a newly introduced system of rationing of events means that they will be kept under tighter control and my guess is that we are going to see Finns at the forefront of speed rallies for a long time to come.

One event which should survive for ever is the Safari, although European entries will always be erratic in number, simply because of the costs involved. It would be difficult for any manufacturer to bear the cost of expensive forays on the Monte, Safari and a Marathon in any one year. The days when manufacturers sent cars tripping gaily around all the major rallies without any thought for their marketing impact have gone. This could affect the future of rallies like the Acropolis, where the domestic market is relatively small. Market research shows convincingly that rallies such as the Austrian Alpine, Acropolis, Thousand Lakes and so on, only get real publicity in their country of origin (with, of course, some mild rub-off in adjacent countries).

It is sad, but inevitable, that rallies like the Tulip and Alpine should die. Inevitable, because the Tulip didn't offer enough to distinguish it from so many other events, while the Alpine became too costly for the publicity rewards and the organisers got out of touch with what the modern competitor wants. Maybe we need a small but highly skilled team of professional organisers going round to all the major rallies, stamping their seal of good organisation on them, particularly over such things as timekeeping, results service and so on. I'm not suggesting that we want all rallies to be stereotyped; far from it. We need every rally to have a character of its own, but at the same time we need a reasonable standard of organisation. At least we do if works teams are going to invest a lot of money in taking part.

It can be argued that you don't need works teams to run a successful rally (as the Circuit of Ireland so often proves—and will have to go on proving while it clashes with so much other Easter sport, including the Safari), but there is no doubt that, if you have works cars, you have well-known drivers. If you have well-known drivers you get more press and television coverage. If you have press and television coverage you have happy sponsors. Happy sponsors come back for more, and there the defence rests.

Incidentally, what a blessing for rallying that any television coverage of it has, by its very nature, to be from film which is edited. I feel that a television film of a rally tends to make more attractive viewing than live coverage of a Saturday afternoon motor race which may, though no fault of the television producer, turn out to be a processional non-event.

Whatever happens to all the other rallies, we must selfishly keep our fingers firmly crossed for the UK's own event—the RAC Rally. Ask any of the Finns or Swedes which is their favourite rally and most of them will name the RAC because of the friendly atmosphere, the great stages and the ban on practising. It seems a pity that such a magnificent event should flirt with financial disaster, largely brought on by the charges made by the Forestry Commission for the use of their tracts for special stages.

It seems misguided that the general committee of the RAC cannot appreciate that they should write-off a reasonable sum each year to support the Rally because of the extensive publicity it gives to the Club. I suspect they would quickly complain if it ever became the AA Rally . . .

Clearly sponsors are becoming as important in rallying as in racing, but drivers must rid themselves of the idea that a sponsor equals someone who gives you money. A sponsor is someone who enters into a business arrangement which should result in him getting as much out of the deal as the driver. If he is a wealthy enthusiast sponsoring a car for fun, then standing by a bedraggled driver at the end of an event may be reward enough; but if the sponsor is a company selling to the public, then the drivers must be prepared to work hard on the promotional side—opening garages, giving talks, addressing sales conferences, doing in-store promotions and generally working as hard as they can to promote the product.

To attract sponsors, it follows that advertising must be completely free on cars and that results for events must be clear-cut. There must be only one overall winner, although slightly more emphasis on class wins than at present wouldn't be such a bad thing. We want the maximum number of sponsors to gain some crumbs from their investment.

More and more organisers are selling their events to sponsors, which is fine provided they don't get too tangled with motor trade sponsorship—clearly a firm like Castrol aren't going to take very big advertising spaces to proclaim the fact that one of their runners has won a rally named after another oil company. Organisers probably stand more chance of getting major sponsors than competitors, because if a sponsor backs an event he really can't lose, but if he backs a competitor then he may see his car in a ditch on the first corner of the rally. A health food is currently quite active in motoring sport—but it won't look too good if their drivers ever have to back out of a rally at the last minute through chilblains!

Incidentally, with clear-cut results on all rallies we also need a World Championship for rallies, to stand alongside the one for Grand Prix racing, although the rally one should be for manufacturers—motor manufacturers are selling cars not drivers.

A World Championship with reasonable interest from works teams will ensure continued support from the unheralded but vital trade people—the oil, tyre, lighting and brake companies and so on, without whom rallying couldn't survive. I suspect that this support in future may swing to a more regional basis, eg Castrol France will have their own budget to support competitions in France and so on, with just an overlay of central interest in classic rallies such as the Monte and RAC.

Stuart Turner patiently supervises the servicing of the winning Escort of Hannu Mikkola and Gunnar Palm on the World Cup Rally.

I seem to have got a long way into this article without having strayed from the promotional side of the sport. I make no apologies for this because, as people have more and more leisure, rallying will be competing for people's attention against a growing variety of attractions . . . private flying has got to increase over the next ten years . . . cheap flights to East Africa are going to pull people to big game watching . . . the hovercraft craze may finally get under way. The counter attractions will be legion, and rallying will have to beat the drum hard to be heard.

Although manufacturers are selling cars not people, rallying still needs its characters (you can't get a car mentioned in the gossip columns of the national newspapers because it's been caught in bed with a Duchess) and we need a much more positive approach to the press coverage given to rallying. I'm bound to upset some (or all) of my fellow contributors to this book, but I dearly wish that rallying had a Denis Jenkinson to chronicle the rally world in the same interesting way in which he covers Formula 1. Rallying suffers from extremes in its press coverage—it gets too little in some motoring magazines which should know better and too much in one or two others.

At the moment rallying is throwing up fewer characters than Formula 1 racing but I suspect that the latter is now getting so expensive and esoteric that the general public have stopped identifying themselves with it. Little boys probably still dream that they are Stirling Moss in their pyjamas styled to look like racing overalls . . . but I doubt if their dads think that Formula 1 cars have got much to do with their bangers in the garage. Rally cars *do* look like production vehicles which is why, if I had to forecast (and that's what this article is supposed to be about), I'd guess that if, say, Porsche ever have to choose between racing and rallying, they'll plump for rallying.

One aspect of the 1971 Safari was much more important than it may have seemed on the surface—the entry of Sears Roebuck into the fray. They not only had a class win to show for their first overseas rally attempt, but they also had several thousand feet of film to take back for television use in the States. If their Safari project is rated by them as a success, as I'm sure it will be, then think what it could do for the sport if it leads to a larger influx of American interest and money.

As far as rally cars of the future are concerned, I am sure that the present Group 2 regulations will eventually change. They are frighteningly expensive, they don't sit very easily alongside several countries' safety regulations, and they mean that cars are a bit too far removed from what people can buy in the showroom.

By 1980, or sooner, rallies will have a standard car or 'showroom' class, which may allow minor modifications like a bit of polishing and certainly a change of brake material, but it won't allow major items to be modified.

However, I don't think we should ban modifications until virtually forced into it by law, because we must never under-estimate the development benefits of rallying. That is why I'd like to think that the trans-continental events will always remain free so that manufacturers can experiment. The public perhaps have a right to expect a normal car to get to Monte Carlo and do a rally without exotic modifications, but no one would seriously expect to drive to Sydney without making some changes to their car, and therefore the public surely expect cars on Marathon events to be special.

Whatever the regulations for rally cars, scrutineering must be simple and sure. Maybe we ought to be sealing more parts at the start of rallies so that an extensive service network plays less part in the results of long events. It is certainly a lost cause to try to ban service, just as it is to stop recceing—much as this would please the drivers who hate to spend so much time trailing backwards and forwards over rally routes.

As far as rally drivers are concerned, I think they are in for a lean time. Business is getting tougher throughout the world, which means that budgets are getting long, hard looks. Which means that there will have to be good commercial reasons for doing rallies. Which means that probably never more than 50 per cent of manufacturers will ever be rallying at any one time. Which means that there are always going to be more drivers than drives available. Which means that driving fees won't get any higher. Pause for a silver collection!

Rally drivers need to watch closely what is happening in Formula 1 racing where, given two drivers of equal ability, the one who gets the drive is the one who carries the most sponsorship. I heartily agree with those who feel that this 'rentadrive' aspect has debased what is supposed to be the pinnacle of motor racing—but it is a fact of life which we have to live with, and one which could happen in rallying.

The present bunch of rally drivers are growing old gracefully together (and not getting any slower in the process!) and I suspect that the Clarks, Makinens and Aaltonens may all drop out of the scene in three or four years time. This will leave a void which will be filled largely by Scandinavians. However, there will always be a need for one or two British drivers and if the present crop of hopefuls persevere and are around in three or four years then there will certainly be opportunities for them. If they've given up hope by then and have dropped out of rallying, then they never had that essential dollop of determination which every good rally driver needs in his make-up.

Whatever the future holds for rallying, there will still be people so hooked on it that they will want to be full-time drivers, whatever the rewards and whatever the prospects for them when they stop. They would probably all like to know the secret of getting a works drive but frankly there isn't one, because every top driver got there through a different route. Most of them had luck; all of them had talent.

I suppose you could always make a point of buying your rally petrol at garages offering trading stamps, then give them to your favourite competition manager. Philately will get you anywhere.

Rally car specifications

THE FOLLOWING technical specifications of rally cars have been selected from those models that have finished in the first three places on a major international rally within the past three years. Also included are those models that are significant class and category winners.

The information listed is that officially quoted by the manufacturer on the form of recognition submitted to the FIA for the homologation of the model.

While it would have been interesting to have included performance figures for these models, it proved impossible to find accurate road tests for the cars in rally tune. Furthermore, the variation of axle ratios, tyre and wheel sizes fitted to rally cars means that it is misleading to quote comparable figures.

Alpine-Renault A110 - 1600

2-seater Group 3 or 4 grand touring car. 4 cylinders, 1,596 cc, 77.8 mm bore, 84 mm stroke. 125 bhp at 6,000 rpm (Group 3), 155 bhp (Group 4). Compression ratio 11.25:1. 5-speed gearbox. Twin Weber carburettors. Wheelbase 2,100 mm, track 1,358 mm (front) 1,337 mm (rear). Overall length 3,845 mm, width 1,520 mm, height 1,120 mm. Weight 650 kg.

Autobianchi A112

4-seater Group 1 or 2 touring car. 4 cylinders, 903 cc, 65 mm bore, 68 mm stroke. 44 bhp at 5,600 rpm (Group 1). Compression ratio 9:1. One Weber carburettor. 4-speed gearbox. Wheelbase 2,038 mm, track 1,250 mm (front) 1,224 mm (rear). Overall length 3,231 mm, width 1,480 mm, height 1,340 mm. Weight 640 kg.

BMW 2002TI

4-seater Group 1 or 2 touring car. 4 cylinders, 1,990 cc, 89 mm bore, 80 mm stroke. 120 bhp at 5,500 rpm (Group 1) 140 bhp (Group 2). Compression ratio 9.3:1. Twin Solex carburettors. 5-speed gearbox. Wheelbase 2,500 mm, track (front and rear) 1,348 mm. Overall length 4,230 mm, width 1,590 mm, height 1,410 mm. Weight 890 kg.

Citroen DS21

4-seater Group 1 or 2 touring car. 4 cylinders, 2,175 cc, 90 mm bore, 85.5 mm stroke. 100 bhp at 6,000 rpm (Group 1). Compression ratio 9:1. Bosch fuel injection. 4-speed gearbox. Wheelbase 3,125 mm, track 1,516 mm (front) 1,316 mm (rear). Overall length 4,874 mm, width 1,803 mm, height 1,470 mm. Weight 1,260 kg.

Daf 55

4-seater Group 1 or 2 touring car. 4 cylinders, 1,108 cc, 70 mm bore, 72 mm stroke. 55 bhp at 5,600 rpm (Group 1), 72 bhp (Group 2). Compression ratio 8.5:1. One Solex carburettor. Variable transmission. Wheelbase 2,250 mm, track 1,280 mm (front) 1,250 mm (rear). Overall length 3,880 mm, width 1,540 mm, height 1,380 mm. Weight 740 kg.

Datsun P510 - 1600SSS

4-seater Group 1 or 2 touring car. 4 cylinders, 1,595 cc, 83 mm bore, 73.7 mm stroke. 100 bhp at 6,000 rpm (Group 1), 120 bhp (Group 2). Compression ratio 9.5:1. Twin Hitachi carburettors. 4-speed gearbox. Wheelbase 2,420 mm, track (front and rear) 1,280 mm. Overall length 4,070 mm, width 1,560 mm, height 1,400 mm. Weight 865 kg.

Datsun 240Z

2-seater Group 3 grand touring car. 6 cylinders, 2,394 cc, 83 mm bore, 73.7 mm stroke. 150 bhp at 6,000 rpm (standard), 230 bhp (Group 3). Compression ratio 9:1. Triple Weber carburettors. 5-speed gearbox. Wheelbase 2,305 mm, track 1,355 mm (front) 1,345 mm (rear). Overall length 4,140 mm, width 1,615 mm, height 1,575 mm. Weight 920 kg.

Ford Escort Twin Cam

4-seater Group 2 touring car. 4 cylinders, 1,558 cc, 82.55 mm bore, 72.75 mm stroke. 115 bhp at 6,000 rpm (standard), 162 bhp (Group 2), 178 bhp (Group 6). Compression ratio 9.8:1. Twin Weber carburettors. 4-speed gearbox. Wheelbase 2,430 mm, track 1,314 mm (front) 1,333 mm (rear). Overall length 3,978 mm, width 1,608 mm, height 1,320 mm. Weight 785 kg.

Ford Escort RS1600

4-seater Group 2 touring car. 4 cylinders, 1,601 cc, 80.97 mm bore, 77.62 mm stroke. 122 bhp at 6,500 rpm (standard), 170 bhp (Group 2), 200 bhp (Group 6). Compression ratio 10.1:1. 4-speed gearbox. Twin Weber carburettors. Wheelbase 2,430 mm, track 1,314 mm (front) 1,333 mm (rear). Overall length 3,978 mm, width 1,608 mm, height 1,320 mm. Weight 790 kg.

Fiat 124 Sport Spider

2-seater Group 3 grand touring car. 4 cylinders, 1,608 cc, 80 mm bore, 80 mm stroke. 110 bhp at 6,400 rpm (standard), 150 bhp (Group 3). Compression ratio 9.8:1. Twin Weber carburettors. 5-speed gearbox. Wheelbase 2,280 mm, track 1,346 mm (front) 1,316 mm (rear). Overall length 3,971 mm, width 1,613 mm, height 1,250 mm. Weight 895 kg.

Lancia Fulvia 1.6HF

2-seater Group 3 grand touring car. 4 cylinders, 1,584 cc, 82 mm bore, 75 mm stroke. 130 bhp at 6,200 rpm (standard), 155 bhp (Group 3). Compression ratio 10.5:1. Twin Weber carburettors. 5-speed gearbox. Wheelbase 2,330 mm, track 1,390 mm (front) 1,335 mm (rear). Overall length 3,935 mm, width 1,605 mm, height 1,300 mm. Weight 780 kg.

Mini-Cooper 'S'

4-seater Group 1 or 2 touring car. 4 cylinders, 1,275 cc, 70.63 mm bore, 81.33 mm stroke. 75 bhp at 5,800 rpm (Group 1), 90 bhp (Group 2). Compression ratio 9.75:1. Twin SU carburettors. 4-speed gearbox. Wheelbase 2,036 mm, track 1,222 mm (front) 1,176 mm (rear). Overall length 3,055 mm, width 1,410 mm, height 1,350 mm. Weight 651 kg.

Moskvitch 412

4-seater Group 1 or 2 touring car. 4 cylinders, 1,480 cc, 82 mm bore, 70 mm stroke. 75 bhp at 5,800 rpm (Group 1). Compression ratio 9:1. One Lenkarz carburettor. 4-speed gearbox. Wheelbase 2,400 mm, track 1,247 mm (front) 1,237 mm (rear). Overall length 4,090 mm, width 1,550 mm, height 1,480 mm. Weight 955 kg.

Opel Rallye Kadett

4-seater Group 1 or 2 touring car. 4 cylinders, 1,897 cc, 93 mm bore, 69.8 mm stroke. 90 bhp at 5,100 rpm (Group 1), 175 bhp (Group 2). Compression ratio 9.5:1. Single Solex carburettor. 4-speed gearbox. Wheelbase 2,146 mm, track 1,252 mm (front) 1,276 mm (rear). Overall length 4,182 mm, width 1,573 mm, height 1,405 mm. Weight 860 kg.

Porsche 911S

2-seater Group 3 grand touring car. 6 cylinders, 2,247 cc, 85 mm bore, 66 mm stroke. 240 bhp at 7,800 rpm. Compression ratio 10.3:1. Bosch fuel injection. 5-speed gearbox. Wheelbase 2,268 mm, track 1,374 mm (front) 1,355 mm (rear). Overall length 4,163 mm, width 1,610 mm, height 1,300 mm. Weight 840 kg.

Porsche 914/6

2-seater Group 4 grand touring car. 6 cylinders, 1,991 cc, 80 mm bore, 66 mm stroke. 220 bhp at 7,800 rpm. Compression ratio 10.3:1. Twin Weber carburettors. 5-speed gearbox. Wheelbase 2,450 mm, track 1,377 mm (front) 1,427 mm (rear). Overall length 3,985 mm, width 1,700 mm, height 1,205 mm. Weight 870 kg.

Saab 96 V4

4-seater Group 1 or 2 touring car. 4 cylinders, 1,698 cc, 90 mm bore, 66.8 mm stroke. 65 bhp at 4,700 rpm (Group 1), 125 bhp (Group 2). Compression ratio 11.5:1. Twin Weber carburettors or Lucas fuel injection. 4-speed gearbox. Wheelbase 2,498 mm, track (front and rear) 1,220 mm. Overall length 4,200 mm, width 1,590 mm, height 1,470 mm. Weight 880 kg.

Skoda S110L

4-seater Group 1 or 2 touring car. 4 cylinders, 1,107 cc, 72 mm bore, 68 mm stroke. 53 bhp at 5,000 rpm (Group 1). Compression ratio 8:1. 4-speed gearbox. Wheelbase 2,400 mm, track 1,280 mm (front) 1,250 mm (rear). Overall length 4,155 mm, width 1,620 mm, height 1,380 mm. Weight 795 kg.

Triumph 2.5PI

4-seater Group 1 or 2 touring car. 6 cylinders, 2,498 cc, 74.7 mm bore, 95 mm stroke. 132 bhp at 5,450 rpm (Group 1). Compression ratio 9.5:1. Lucas fuel injection. 4-speed gearbox. Wheelbase 2,690 mm, track 1,320 mm (front) 1,280 mm (rear). Overall length 4,415 mm, width 1,650 mm, height 1,420 mm. Weight 1143 kg.

APPENDIX 2

International rally drivers and co-drivers

THE FOLLOWING SELECTION of biographies of drivers and co-drivers has been made on the basis of those who have gained consistent successes over the past three years in significant international events.

Most drivers are notoriously modest when it comes to revealing details of their personal background and former achievements. Furthermore, very few manufacturers provide accurate and comprehensive biographies of their team members.

The following information has been gleaned from all known sources, and if any driver has any complaints then probably he has only himself to blame!

We have shown each driver's current marque allegiance according to his 1971 contract. Where no contract details are given it indicates that the driver is either a freelance or is operating with a private sponsor.

Rauno Aaltonen

FINNISH, born 7.1.38 in Turku. Married with two children, lives in Geneva. Former speedboat champion and speedway rider. Started motor racing 1956. Joined BMC team 1962 after works drives with Mercedes. Left BMC 1968 to freelance with Ford, Lancia and Datsun. Major successes: 1961 1st Polish, 1st 1000 Lakes, 2nd German (with Mercedes). 1963 1st Alpine. 1964 1st Liege. 1965 1st Geneva, 1st Czech, 1st Polish, 1st Three Cities, 1st RAC. 1965 European Rally Champion. 1966 1st Tulip, 1st Czech, 3rd Alpine. 1967 1st Monte, 3rd Swedish, 3rd Tulip. 1968 3rd Monte. 1969 2nd Flowers. 1970 3rd World Cup Rally. Current contract: Datsun.

102

Aake Andersson

SWEDISH, born 16.9.40. Married with one daughter. Works in his father's brewery in Rasbo, near Upsala. Started rallying in 1959 with Saab, drove in Saab works team 1963-67 then joined Svenska Volkswagen and Porsche. Major successes: 1965 2nd Swedish. 1966 1st Swedish. 1968 1st Gulf London. Current contract: Porsche.

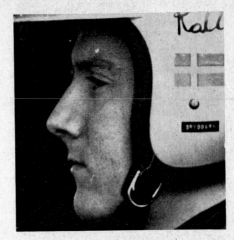

Ove Andersson

SWEDISH, born 1938, lives in Upsala. Married to Elizabeth Nystrom. Former mechanic, drove for BMC Sweden 1963, joined Saab 1964-65, Lancia 1967, Ford 1968 and Alpine-Renault 1971. Major successes: 1966 3rd Monte, 3rd Flowers. 1967 2nd Monte, 3rd Flowers, 2nd Acropolis, 1st Spanish, 1st Gulf London. 1968 3rd Flowers, 2nd Tulip. 1969 1st Welsh. 1970 3rd Acropolis. 1971 1st Monte, 1st San Remo, 1st Austrian Alpine, 1st Acropolis. Current contract: Alpine-Renault.

Jean-Claude Andruet

FRENCH, born 1941, lives in Paris. Started racing Renault in 1965, winning Novices National Championship. Switched to rallying in 1966 driving works Renault Gordini. Joined Alpine team in 1968, winning Index at Le Mans with J-P. Nicolas. Major successes: 1968 1st Lyons-Charbonnieres. 1969 2nd Alpine. 1970 1st Polish, 1st Three Cities, 1st Geneva. 1970 European Rally Champion. 1971 3rd Monte. Current contract: Alpine-Renault.

Stig Blomqvist

SWEDISH, born 29.7.46. Lives in Lindesberg where he runs a driving school. Started rallying in 1964, having navigated for his father in rallies since the age of 12. Joined Saab team in 1968. Major successes: 1970 2nd Swedish. 1971 1st Swedish, 1st Finnish Hanki Rally. 1971 Scandinavian Snow Champion. Current contract: Saab.

Roger Clark

BRITISH, born 5.8.39. Lives in Narborough, Leicestershire. Married with one son. Garage proprietor. Started rallying in 1956 with Ford Thames van, then Renault Dauphine and Mini. First international 1963, drove for Rover in 1964, member of Ford works team from 1966 to date. Major successes: 1964 1st Scottish, 1st Welsh, 1st Gulf London. 1965 1st Scottish, 3rd Circuit. 1966 2nd Acropolis, 2nd Alpine. 1967 1st Scottish. 1968 1st Circuit, 1st Tulip. 1st Shell 4000, 1st Acropolis, 1st Scottish. 1969 1st Circuit, 2nd Acropolis. 1970 1st Circuit. Current contract: Ford.

Andrew Cowan

SCOTTISH, born 13.12.36. Single. Lives at Duns, Berwickshire. Farmer and director of rally driving school in Australia. Started rallying in 1959 with Sunbeam Rapier, first international 1961. Drove for Rootes till 1969 then, after winning London-Sydney Marathon, joined British Leyland. Major successes: 1961 1st Scottish. 1962 1st Scottish. 1964 1st category Tour de France. 1966 1st Welsh. 1968 1st London-Sydney Marathon. 1969 1st Southern Cross.

Brian Culcheth

BRITISH, born 3.8.38 in London. Single, lives in Sandy, Bedfordshire. Worked as clerk in Daily Mirror office, then car salesman and sales director of north London garage. Started rallying in 1959 with Sprite and Mini. Joined BMC team in 1967. Major successes: 1970 2nd World Cup Rally, 1st Scottish.

Tony Fall

BRITISH, born 23.3.40. Married with one son. Lives in Shipley, Yorkshire. Former car salesman, started rallying in 1964, joined BMC team in 1966. Drove for Lancia in 1968 and has since freelanced with Ford, Porsche, Datsun and BMW. Major successes: 1966 1st Circuit, 1st Scottish, 2nd Geneva, 1st Polish. 1967 3rd Geneva, 1st Danube (all with BMC). 1968 1st TAP (with Lancia). 1969 1st Rally of Incas (with Ford), 3rd RAC (with Lancia.) 1971 1st Welsh (with Datsun).

Edgar Herrmann

BAVARIAN, born 20.2.32. Married with three children, lives in Malindi, Kenya. Hotelier and travel operator. Best known for his Safari record, having driven in this event since 1962 with Mercedes, Ford, Porsche and Datsun. Major successes: 1970 1st Safari, 1st Ampol Trial. 1971 1st Safari. Current contract: Datsun.

Nigel Hollier

BRITISH, born 26.5.43. Married, lives at Sutton Coldfield, Warwickshire. Started rallying in 1968 with Mini and Ford Cortina, now running privately sponsored works Alpine. Major successes: 1970 3rd Castrol-Danube Rally.

Paddy Hopkirk

IRISH, born 14.4.33 in Belfast. Married with two children. Lives in London. Director of car accessory company. Started competitive motoring sport while at Trinity College, Dublin. Joined Standard-Triumph works team in 1956, Rootes in 1958 and BMC in 1962. Major successes: 1961 3rd Alpine. 1962 3rd Monte, 2nd RAC. 1963 2nd Tulip. 1964 1st Monte, 1st Austrian. 1965 1st Circuit. 1966 1st Austrian, 3rd Acropolis. 1967 2nd Flowers, 1st Circuit, 1st Acropolis, 1st Alpine. 1968 2nd London-Sydney Marathon. 1969 2nd Circuit. 1970 2nd Scottish.

Harry Kallstrom

SWEDISH, born 30.6.39. Single. Driving school instructor. Won 1959 Swedish 'T' Rally Championship. 1969 European Rally Champion. Has driven Minis, VWs and, more recently, Lancia works cars. Major successes: 1963 2nd RAC. 1964 2nd Swedish. 1966 2nd RAC. 1969 1st Flowers, 2nd Austrian, 2nd Czech, 3rd Polish, 1st Spanish, 1st RAC. 1970 2nd San Remo, 1st RAC, 2nd Czech. 1971 3rd Swedish. Current contract: Lancia.

Simo Lampinen

FINNISH, born 22.6.43. Married, lives in Porvoo. Started rallying in 1961 after remarkable recovery from polio. Finnish Rally Champion 1963-64. Has driven with works teams for Saab, Ford, Daf, BMC, Standard-Triumph and Lancia. Major successes: 1963 1st 1000 Lakes. 1964 1st 1000 Lakes. 1966 2nd Swedish. 1967 2nd Swedish, 2nd 1000 Lakes. 1968 2nd Czech, 2nd 1000 Lakes, 1st RAC. 1969 2nd Swedish, 1st Scottish, 2nd 1000 Lakes. 1970 3rd 1000 Lakes, 1st TAP. 1971 3rd Acropolis. Current contract: Lancia.

Gerard Larrousse

FRENCH, born 23.5.40, in Lyon. Married, lives in Paris. Started rallying with Alpine in 1968 and moved to Porsche in 1969 for rallies and races. Major successes: 1968 1st Niege et Glace, 1st Rallye Lorraine. 1969 1st Tour de France, 1st Tour de Corse, 2nd Monte. 1970 2nd Monte. Current contract: Porsche.

Hakan Lindberg

SWEDISH, born 18.12.38. Started rallying in 1963 with Opel, then switched to Renault (1965-6), Saab (1967-70) and currently drives for Fiat. Major successes: 1968 1st Norwegian, 3rd Swedish. 1969 1st Norwegian. 1970 2nd Austrian. Current contract: Fiat.

Timo Makinen

FINNISH, born 18.3.38 in Helsinki. Married with one son. Started rallying 1959 with Triumph TR3, and gained support from local BMC dealer for rallying Mini in 1962. Joined BMC works team in 1963, then drove Lancia in 1969 and Ford from 1970. Won Round Britain Power Boat Race in 1968. Major successes: 1964 1st Tulip, 2nd RAC. 1965 1st Monte, 3rd Tulip, 2nd Alpine, 1st 1000 Lakes, 2nd RAC. 1966 2nd Polish, 1st 1000 Lakes, 1st Three Cities. 1967 2nd Tulip, 1st 1000 Lakes (all with BMC). 1970 2nd 1000 Lakes (with Ford). Current contract: Ford.

Hannu Mikkola

FINNISH, born 24.5.42, in Joënsun. Single. Son of timber company director. After university studies as mechanical engineer, started rallying in 1963 with Volvo. Drove works Volvo in 1966, finishing 2nd in Finnish Championship. Drove Lancia 1967 and joined Ford in 1968. Major successes: 1968 1st 1000 Lakes, 2nd Austrian. 1969 1st Austrian, 1st 1000 Lakes. 1970 1st 1000 Lakes, 1st World Cup Rally. Current contract: Ford.

Sandro Munari

ITALIAN, born 27.3.40. Single. 1967 Italian Rally Champion and works Lancia driver. Had bad Monte accident in 1968 when co-driver killed; returned in 1969 to again win Italian Championship. Major successes: 1967 2nd Geneva, 2nd Spanish, 1st Tour de Corse. 1969 1st Sestriere, 1st San Martino di Castrozza. 1970 2nd TAP. Current contract: Lancia.

Lillebror Nasenius

SWEDISH, born 24.11.40. Married with three children. Haulage contractor. Major successes: 1966 European Rally Champion (Group 1), Swedish Rally Champion (Group 1), 3rd Three Cities. 1967 Swedish Rally Champion (Group 1), 2nd Polish. 1968 and 1969 Swedish Rally Champion (Group 1). 1970 3rd RAC. Current contract: Opel.

Jean-Pierre Nicolas

FRENCH, born 1944. Married with one child, lives in Marseilles. Started rallying 1963 in Renault Dauphine with his father (an ex-Renault works driver). Joined Alpine works team in 1968. Major successes: 1963 1st Rally Mistral. 1964 1st Rally Mistral. 1966 1st Madeira Rally. 1967 1st Jean Behra Criterium, 1st Morocco. 1970 3rd Monte, 2nd Geneva, 2nd Three Cities. 1971 2nd Acropolis. Current contract: Alpine-Renault.

Carl Orrenius

SWEDISH, born 23.2.36. Married with three children, lives in Nacka, near Stockholm. Works in family business making bottle tops. Started rallying with Saab in 1956. Major successes: 1960 2nd Tulip. 1967 3rd Scottish. 1968 2nd RAC. 1969 3rd Austrian, 2nd RAC. Current contract: Saab.

Jean-Francois Piot

FRENCH, born 28.3.38. Married with one son, lives in Paris. Studied architecture at university but now runs a garage. Started rallying in 1962 with Renault, then joined Ford France. Major successes: 1967 1st Flowers, 1st Three Cities. 1970 3rd Austrian. Current contract: Ford.

Chris Sclater

BRITISH, born 31.12.45 in Sussex. Single, lives in London and works as an engineer. Started rallying in 1966 with Ford Anglia. Major successes: 1970 2nd Circuit, 2nd Welsh, 1st Manx, 2nd RAC Rally Championship. 1971 2nd Circuit, 1st Scottish (all with Ford).

Joginder Singh

INDIAN, born 9.2.32, lives in Nairobi. One of eight sons whose father settled in East Africa from India and started a garage business. Began rallying in 1958. Won Kenya Rally Championship in 1966, 1969 and 1970, and East African Rally Championship in 1965 and 1970. Has finished every Safari Rally since 1959, driving VW, Volvo, Fiat, Datsun and Ford. Major successes: 1965 1st Safari. 1966 3rd Safari. 1969 2nd Safari. 1970 2nd Safari.

Rosemary Smith

IRISH, born 7.8.37, in Dublin. Married, lives on farm near Dublin. Former dress designer, first rallied in 1960 with a Mini. Joined Rootes team in 1961 and later drove Ford and British Leyland. Won 1965 Tulip Rally outright and ladies' prize on following events: Tour de France (twice), Circuit of Ireland (five times), Scottish Rally (six times), Canadian Shell 4000 (twice), Monte Carlo, Acropolis and World Cup Rally.

Will Sparrow

BRITISH, born 1945. Motor engineer from Solihull, Warwickshire. Started rallying in 1962 in Mini van, and has subsequently always rallied a Mini. 1970 RAC Rally Champion. Major successes: 1970 1st Welsh. 1971 2nd Welsh.

Gilbert Staepelaere

BELGIAN, born 5.6.37 in Antwerp. Married with three children. Started navigating for his father in rallies in 1953, first event as driver in 1959. Belgian National Rally Champion in 1964. Major successes: 1961 1st Tour de Belgique. 1966 1st Geneva, 1st Tour de Belgique. 1968 3rd Czech. 1969 1st Tulip, 1st Czech, 2nd Polish, 2nd Spanish. 1970 1st Czech, 3rd Polish, 3rd Three Cities (all with Ford). Current contract: Ford.

Jean-Luc Therier

FRENCH, born 1945 in Normandy. Lives at Neufchatel-in-Braye, near Dieppe. Started racing Renault Gordini 1966, and won first rally in 1967. Won efficiency index at Le Mans in 1968 with Alpine, and joined works Renault team. Major successes: 1970 1st San Remo, 1st Acropolis. 1971 2nd Monte. Current contract: Alpine-Renault.

Pauli Toivonen

FINNISH, born 22.8.29 in Jyväskylä. Married with two children. Head of firm importing car radios. Scandinavian Rally Champion in 1962 with Citroen. European Rally Champion in 1968 with Porsche. Major successes: 1961 2nd 1000 Lakes. 1962 1st 1000 Lakes. 1963 2nd Monte. 1965 3rd 1000 Lakes. 1966 1st Monte (all with Citroen). 1968 2nd Monte, 1st San Remo, 1st East German, 1st West German, 3rd Acropolis, 1st Castrol-Danube. 1969 1st Acropolis (all with Porsche).

Tom Trana

SWEDISH, born 29.11.37 in Kristinehamn. Married, lives in Gothenburg and works in Saab test department. Came from a motoring family, started rallying in 1956 with Volvo. European Rally Champion 1964 with Volvo, and Swedish Rally Champion 1966 and 1968. Joined Saab works team in 1967. Major successes: 1963 1st RAC. 1964 1st Acropolis, 1st Swedish, 1st RAC. 1965 1st Swedish. 1966 3rd Swedish, 2nd 1000 Lakes, 3rd RAC. 1967 1st Norwegian. 1968 2nd Swedish, 2nd Norwegian. 1969 3rd Norwegian. Current contract: Saab.

Jean Vinatier

FRENCH, born 1935. Has been racing and rallying for 20 years, starting with Panhard and DB. Joined Renault works team in 1962. Major successes: 1961 Index win in Tour de France. 1964 1st Tour de Corse. 1967 2nd Danube. 1968 1st Czech, 1st Alpine, 1st Criterium des Cevennes, 1st Vercors Rally. 1969 3rd Monte, 1st Alpine, 2nd Three Cities. 1970 3rd San Remo, 2nd Acropolis.

Bjorn Waldegaard

SWEDISH, born 12.11.43. Married with one child, lives in Rimbo. Swedish Rally Champion in 1968-69 with Porsche. Major successes: 1968 1st Swedish. 1969 1st Monte, 1st Swedish. 1970 1st Monte, 1st Swedish. 1st Austrian, 3rd TAP. 1971 3rd Monte. Current contract: Porsche.

Sobieslav Zasada

POLISH, lives in Krakow. Made his name driving Steyr Puch, more recently driven Ford and Porsche. Won European Rally Championship in 1966 (Porsche Group 2) and 1967 (Porsche Group 1). Major successes: 1961 1st Polish. 1964 1st Polish. 1965 3rd Geneva, 2nd Polish. 1966 3rd Polish. 1967 3rd Lyon-Charbonnieres, 1st Austrian, 2nd Czech, 1st Polish. 1968 2nd East German, 2nd West German, 2nd Acropolis. 1969 1st Polish. 1970 2nd Polish.

Co-drivers

John Davenport

BRITISH, born 21.11.39. Married, lives in London. Rally editor of Autosport, started rallying as co-driver in 1963. Driven with Rover, Saab, Ford and Lancia works teams. Major successes: 1966 2nd Tulip (with Vic Elford). 1967 2nd Monte, 3rd Flowers, 2nd Acropolis, 1st Spanish.1968 3rd Flowers, 2nd Tulip (all with O. Andersson), 1st RAC. 1970 3rd 1000 Lakes, 1st TAP. 1971 3rd Acropolis (with S. Lampinen), 1st Scottish (with C. Sclater). Current contract: Lancia.

Paul Easter

BRITISH, born 12.1.39. Married with one daughter. Lives in Old Stratford, Buckinghamshire. Garage proprietor. Started rallying as driver in 1961 with Mini. Member of BMC team from 1964-68 as co-driver to Timo Makinen. Later co-driver with Timo Makinen (BMW and Ford) and Rauno Aaltonen (Datsun). Major successes: 1965 1st Monte, 3rd Tulip, 2nd Alpine, 2nd RAC. 1966 3rd Czech, 2nd Polish, 1st Three Cities. 1967 2nd Tulip.

Gunnar Haggbom

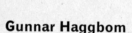

SWEDISH, born 7.12.35. Married with two children. Worked as accountant with Swedish BMC agent. Started co-driving in 1959 with Harry Kallstrom, also partnering Gunnar Andersson and Eric Carlsson. Won European Rally Championship with Kallstrom in 1969. Major successes: 1962 1st Monte, 3rd Swedish, 3rd 1000 Lakes, 2nd Geneva (all with Carlsson). 1963 2nd RAC. 1969 1st Flowers, 2nd Austrian, 2nd Czech, 3rd Polish, 1st Spanish, 1st RAC. 1970 2nd San Remo, 1st RAC, 2nd Czech. 1971 3rd Swedish (all with Kallstrom). Current contract: Lancia.

Henry Liddon

BRITISH, born London 20.4.32. Married with two daughters. Lives in Bristol. Photographer and car salesman before turning professional co-driver. Started rallying in 1952, member of BMC team 1963-68, then with Lancia and currently Ford. Major successes: 1963 2nd Tulip. 1964 1st Monte, 1st Austrian (with Paddy Hopkirk). 1966 1st Circuit (with Tony Fall). 1st Tulip, 1st Czech, 3rd Alpine. 1967 1st Monte, 3rd Swedish, 3rd Tulip. 1968 3rd Monte. 1969 2nd Flowers (all with Aaltonen). 3rd RAC (with Fall). 1970 2nd 1000 Lakes (with Makinen) 3rd World Cup Rally (with Aaltonen). Current contract: Ford.

Tony Nash

BRITISH, born 21.2.34 in Watten, Somerset. Married with one daughter. Lives in Bristol. Garage proprietor, started club rallying in 1955, joined BMC team in 1962, then retired from rallying in 1964. Joined British Leyland team in 1968 as regular co-driver to Paddy Hopkirk. Major successes: 1969 2nd Circuit, 2nd TAP, 2nd London-Sydney Marathon. 1970 2nd Scottish. 1971 1st Flowers (with Ove Andersson).

Gunnar Palm

SWEDISH, born 25.2.37 in Kristinehamn. Single. An ardent sportsman, former speedway rider, ski-jumper and ice hockey player. Started rallying in 1957, first international in 1961. Drove with Eric Carlsson 1963-4 and Ford team from 1966. Major successes: 1963 1st Monte, 2nd Swedish, 2nd Liege, 3rd RAC. 1964 3rd Monte, 1st Flowers, 2nd Safari, 2nd Polish, 2nd Alpine, 2nd Liege, 3rd Geneva (all with Carlsson). 1966 1st Acropolis, 2nd Czech, 1st RAC. 1967 1st Swedish, 3rd Acropolis, 2nd Three Cities. 1968 1st Austrian, 3rd 1000 Lakes (all with Bengt Soderstrom). 1970 1st 1000 Lakes, 1st World Cup Rally (with Hannu Mikkola). Current contract: Ford.

Jim Porter

BRITISH, born 9.11.39 in Leicester. Married. Left family cattle buying and meat producing company to become professional co-driver. Started rallying in 1956, teamed up with Roger Clark in 1958, joined Ford in 1965. Major successes: 1965 1st Scottish, 3rd Circuit. 1967 1st Scottish. 1968 1st Circuit, 1st Tulip, 1st Acropolis, 1st Scottish. 1969 1st Circuit, 2nd Acropolis. 1970 3rd Acropolis. Current contract: Ford.

David Stone

BRITISH, born 10.2.40 in South Wales. Married. Managing director of catering group, lives in Bristol. Started rallying in 1956, club rallies with Pat Moss. Later teamed up with Eric Carlsson, Vic Elford, Sandro Munari, J. P. Nicolas and Ove Andersson. Major successes: 1962 1st RAC. 1963 3rd Tulip. 1964 1st Alpine, 3rd RAC. 1965 3rd Circuit. 1966 3rd Corsica. 1967 1st Lyon-Charbonnieres, 1st Tulip, 1st Geneva, 3rd Corsica, 3rd Monte. 1968 1st Monte. 1969 2nd RAC. 1970 1st Lyon-Charbonnieres, 1st Spanish, 2nd Acropolis. 1971 1st Monte.

Michael Wood

BRITISH, born 20.1.34. Married with two children. Lives in Burnley, Lancashire. Started rallying in 1953 as driver and navigator, won BTRDA Gold Star 1955-56. First international 1955, joined BMC team 1965-68 as regular co-driver with Tony Fall. Joined Ford team in 1969 and returned to partner Fall with Datsun, Lancia and BMW in 1971. Major successes: 1966 1st Scottish. 1967 1st Danube, 3rd Geneva (with Fall). 1968 3rd Tulip (with Julien Vernaeve). 1969 1st Austrian (with Hannu Mikkola). 1971 1st Welsh (with Tony Fall).

116

APPENDIX 3

International rally results

IT HAS NOT BEEN an easy task to select which events should be included in the following pages, which cover the results of the major international rallies since 1960.

Generally, all the European Rally Championship qualifying rounds have been included, along with significant non-Championship events, such as the East African Safari. Events of particular interest to British enthusiasts, such as the Circuit of Ireland and the Scottish Rally, have been included since 1965 when they became truly international.

Many rally organisers and reporters are notoriously inaccurate when it comes to documenting the results of some of the more obscure events and, despite a lot of cross-checking, the following record is still not complete in every detail. If anyone is able to make any corrections, or indeed to find any mistakes, please let us know so that we can keep the record straight.

1960

Monte Carlo Rally
1 W. Schock/R. Moll—Mercedes 220SE
2 E. Bohringer/H. Socher—Mercedes 220SE
3 R. Ott/E. Mahle—Mercedes 220SE

East African Safari
1 W. Fritschy/J. Ellis—Mercedes 219
2 M. Temple-Boreham/Mrs. Temple-Boreham—Citroen ID19
3 V. Preston/J. Harrison—Ford Zephyr

Geneva Rally
1 R. de Lageneste/H. Greder—Alfa Romeo 1300
2 R. Trautmann/J. Ogier—Citroen
3 . Schild/ . Briffaud—Alfa Romeo

Tulip Rally
1 R. Trautmann/G. Verrier—Citroen ID19
2 C. Orrenius/R. Dahlgren—Saab 96
3 W. Schock/R. Moll—Mercedes 220SE

Acropolis Rally
1 W. Schock/R. Moll—Mercedes 220SE
2 E. Carlsson/W. Karlsson—Saab 95
3 W. Levy/ . Linzenberger—Auto Union

Swedish Midnight Sun Rally
1 C. Skogh/R. Skogh—Saab 96
2 H. Bengtsson/ E. Petterson—Porsche S90
3 G. Andersson/C. Lohmander—Volvo 544

Alpine Rally
1 R. de Lageneste/H. Greder—Alfa Romeo Giulietta
2 P. Moss/A. Wisdom—Austin-Healey 3000
3 J. Behra/R. Richard—Jaguar 3.8

Finnish 1000 Lakes Rally
1 C. Bremer/J. Lampi—Saab 96
2 E. Carlsson/L. Simonsson—Saab 96
3 C. Skogh/R. Skogh—Saab 96

Liège-Rome-Liège Rally
1 P. Moss/A. Wisdom—Austin-Healey 3000
2 G. Sander/W. Sander—Porsche S90
3 J. Sprinzel/J. Patten—Austin-Healey Sprite

Polish Rally
1 W. Schock/R. Moll—Mercedes 220SE
2 C. Bremer/J. Lampi—Saab 96
3 K. Otto/H. Hampf—Wartburg

Viking Rally
1 C. Skogh/R. Skogh—Saab 96
2 . Wernersson/ . Nilsson—Saab 96
3 G. Andersson/ . Floysvik—Volvo 544S

German Rally
1 G. Andersson/W. Karlsson—Volvo 544S
2 R. Trautmann/J. Ogier—Citroen ID19
3 R. Kreder/R. Knoll—Mercedes 190B

RAC Rally
1 E. Carlsson/S. Turner—Saab 96
2 J. Sprinzel/R. Bensted-Smith—
   Austin-Healey Sprite
3 D. Morley/E. Morley—Austin-Healey 3000

1961

Monte Carlo Rally
1 M. Martin/R. Bateau—Panhard
2 W. Loffler/H. Walter—Panhard
3 G. Jouanneaux/A. Coquillet—Panhard

East African Safari
1 C. Manussis/W. Coleridge—Mercedes 220SE
2 W. Fritschy/K. Mandeville—Mercedes 220SE
3 A. Hall/L. Cardwell—Ford Zephyr

Tulip Rally
1 G. Mabbs/L. Griffiths—Triumph Herald
2 H. Walter/W. Schock—Porsche Carrera
3 C. Skogh/R. Skogh—Saab 96

Acropolis Rally
1 E. Carlsson/W. Karlsson—Saab 96
2 G. Andersson/C. Lohmander—Volvo 544
3 P. Riley/A. Ambrose—Austin-Healey 3000

Swedish Midnight Sun Rally
1 C. Skogh/R. Skogh—Saab 96
2 B. Soderstrom/B. Olsson—Volkswagen
3 . Wernersson/ . Jonsson—Saab 96

Alpine Rally
1 D. Morley/E. Morley—Austin-Healey 3000
2 J. Rolland/G. Augias—Alfa Romeo Giulietta
3 P. Hopkirk/J. Scott—Sunbeam Rapier

Polish Rally
1 E. Bohringer/R. Aaltonen—Mercedes 220SE
2 C. Skogh/K. Svensson—Saab
3 S. Zasada/E. Zasada—BMW 700

Finnish 1000 Lakes Rally
1 R. Aaltonen/ . Nurminaa—Mercedes 220SE
2 P. Toivonen/J. Kallio—Citroen
3 E. Keinanen/R. Eklund—Skoda

Liège-Sofia-Liège Rally
1 L. Bianchi/G. Harris—Citroen DS 19
2 H. Walter/H. Wencher—Porsche
3 R. Neyret/J. Terramorsi—Citroen ID19

German Rally
1 H. Walter/H. Wencher—Porsche Carrera
2 E. Bohringer/R. Aaltonen—Mercedes 220SE
3 G. Andersson/W. Karlsson—Volvo

RAC Rally
1 E. Carlsson/J. Brown—Saab 96
2 P. Moss/A. Wisdom—Austin-Healey 3000
3 P. Harper/I. Hall—Sunbeam Rapier

1962

Monte Carlo Rally
1 E. Carlsson/G. Haggbom—Saab 96
2 E. Bohringer/P. Lang—Mercedes 220SE
3 P. Hopkirk/J. Scott—Sunbeam Rapier

East African Safari
1 T. Fjastad/W. Schmider—Volkswagen
2 N. Nowicki/P. Cliff—Peugeot 404
3 P. Moss/A. Wisdom—Saab

Tulip Rally
1 P. Moss/A. Wisdom—Mini-Cooper
2 G. Andersson/W. Karlsson—Volvo 544
3 P. Gele/C. Laurent—DKW Junior

Acropolis Rally
1 E. Bohringer/P. Lang—Mercedes 220SE
2 E. Carlsson/K. Svensson—Saab 96
3 R. Trautmann/L. Herve—Citroen DS19

Alpine Rally
1 D. Morley/E. Morley—Austin-Healey 3000
2 H. Walter/K. Shottler—Porsche Carrera
3 P. Moss/P. Mayman—Austin-Healey 3000

Swedish Midnight Sun Rally
1 B. Soderstrom/B. Olsson—Mini-Cooper
2 H. Bengtsson/R. Dahlgren—Porsche
3 E. Carlsson/G. Haggbom—Saab 96

Polish Rally
1 E. Bohringer/P. Lang—Mercedes 220SE
2 P. Moss/P. Mayman—Austin-Healey 3000
3 H. Kuhne/H. Wencher—Mercedes 220SE

Finnish 1000 Lakes Rally
1 P. Toivonen/J. Kallio—Citroen DS19
2 E. Keinanen/R. Eklund—Skoda
3 E. Carlsson/G. Haggbom—Saab 96

Liège-Sofia-Liège Rally
1 E. Bohringer/H. Eger—Mercedes 220SE
2 H. Marang/P. Coltelloni—Citroen DS19
3 J. Patte/P. Rouselle—Volvo B18

German Baden-Baden Rally
1 P. Moss/P. Mayman—Mini-Cooper
2 E. Bohringer/P. Lang—Mercedes 220SE
3 R. Trautmann/C. Bouchet—Citroen DS19

Geneva Rally
1 H. Walter/W. Lier—Porsche Carrera
2 E. Carlsson/G. Haggbom—Saab
3 P. Moss/P. Mayman—Mini-Cooper

RAC Rally
1 E. Carlsson/D. Stone—Saab 96
2 P. Hopkirk/J. Scott—Austin-Healey 3000
3 P. Moss/P. Mayman—Austin-Healey 3000

1963

Monte Carlo Rally
1 E. Carlsson/G. Palm—Saab 96
2 P. Toivonen/A. Jarvi—Citroen DS19
3 R. Aaltonen/A. Ambrose—Mini-Cooper

East African Safari
1 N. Nowicki/P. Cliff—Peugeot 404
2 P. Hughes/W. Young—Ford Anglia
3 J. Cardwell/W. Lead—Mercedes 220SE

Tulip Rally
Touring Category
1 H. Greder/M. Delalande—Ford Falcon
2 P. Hopkirk/H. Liddon—Mini-Cooper
3 G. Andersson/L. Berggren—Volvo 122S

Grand Touring
1 L. Bakker/H. Umbach—Porsche S90
2 D. Morley/E. Morley—Austin-Healey 3000
3 J. Vernaeve/H. Vittel—Mini-Cooper

Acropolis Rally
1 E. Bohringer/R. Kroll—Mercedes 300SE
2 G. Andersson/W. Karlsson—Volvo 122
3 C. Skogh/L. Berggren—Volvo 122

Swedish Midnight Sun Rally
1 B. Jansson/E. Petterson—Porsche S90
2 E. Carlsson/G. Palm—Saab Sport
3 B. Ljungfeldt/B. Rehnfeldt—Ford Cortina GT

Alpine Rally
1 R. Aaltonen/A. Ambrose—Mini-Cooper 'S'
2 J. Rolland/G. Augias—Alfa Romeo Giulietta
3 H. Taylor/B. Melia—Ford Cortina GT

Spa-Sofia-Liège Rally
1 E. Bohringer/K. Kaiser—Mercedes 230SL
2 E. Carlsson/G. Palm—Saab Sport
3 L. Bianchi/J. Ogier—Citroen DS19

RAC Rally
1 T. Trana/S. Lindstrom—Volvo 544
2 H. Kallstrom/G. Haggbom—
   Volkswagen 1500S
3 E. Carlsson/G. Palm—Saab Sport

1964

Monte Carlo Rally
1 P. Hopkirk/H. Liddon—Mini-Cooper 'S'
2 B. Ljungfeldt/F. Sager—Ford Falcon
3 E. Carlsson/G. Palm—Saab Sport

Italian Flowers Rally
1 E. Carlsson/G. Palm—Saab 96
2 P. Moss/V. Domleo—Saab 96
3 . Frescobaldi/D. Innocenti—Lancia Flavia

East African Safari
1 P. Hughes/W. Young—Ford Cortina GT
2 E. Carlsson/G. Palm—Saab 96
3 M. Armstrong/C. Bates—Ford Cortina GT

Austrian Alpine Rally
1 P. Hopkirk/H. Liddon—Austin-Healey 3000
2 J. Ortner/—Steyr-Puch
3 A. Cavallari/ . Rubrieri—Alfa Romeo Giulia

Polish Rally
1 S. Zasada/E. Zasada—Steyr-Puch
2 E. Carlsson/G. Palm—Saab 96
3 P. Moss/E. Nystrom—Saab 96

Tulip Rally
Touring category
1 T. Makinen/A. Ambrose—Mini-Cooper 'S'
2 H. Greder/M. Delalande—Ford Falcon
3 C. Skogh/L. Berggren—Volvo 122S

Grand Touring category
1 D. Morley/E. Morley—Austin-Healey 3000
2 B. Jansson/E. Petterson/Porsche Carrera
3 H. Taylor/B. Melia—Ford Cortina GT

Acropolis Rally
1 T. Trana/G. Thermenius—Volvo 544
2 J. Ogier/B. Groll—Citroen DS19
3 P. Moss/V. Domleo—Saab 96

Swedish Midnight Sun Rally
1 T. Trana/G. Thermenius—Volvo 544
2 H. Kallstrom/R. Hakansson—
   Mini-Cooper 'S'
3 B. Soderstrom/B. Olsson—Ford Cortina GT

Alpine Rally
Touring category
1 V. Elford/D. Stone—Ford Cortina GT
2 E. Carlsson/G. Palm—Saab 96
3 J. Ogier/L. Pointet—Citroen DS19

Grand Touring category
1 J. Rolland/G. Augias—Alfa Romeo Giulia
2 D. Morley/E. Morley—Austin-Healey 3000
3 J. Rey/J. Hanrioud—Porsche 904GTS

Spa-Sofia-Liège Rally
1 R. Aaltonen/A. Ambrose—
   Austin-Healey 3000
2 E. Carlsson/G. Palm—Saab Sport
3 E. Bohringer/K. Kaiser—Mercedes 230SL

Geneva Rally
1 H. Greder/M. Delalande—Ford Falcon
2 T. Hunter/P. Lier—Triumph Spitfire
3 E. Carlsson/G. Palm—Saab 96

RAC Rally
1 T. Trana/G. Thermenius—Volvo 544
2 T. Makinen/D. Barrow—Austin-Healey 3000
3 V. Elford/D. Stone—Ford Cortina GT

1965

Monte Carlo Rally
1 T. Makinen/P. Easter—Mini-Cooper 'S'
2 E. Bohringer/R. Wutherich—
    Porsche 904GTS
3 P. Moss/E. Nystrom—Saab

Italian Rally of the Flowers
1 L. Cella/ . Gamenara—Lancia Fulvia
2 L. Tarramazzo/ . Ramoino—Lancia Fulvia
3 B. Jansson/ . Liljedahl—Renault Gordini R8

Swedish Midnight Sun Rally
1 T. Trana/G. Thermenius—Volvo 544
2 A. Andersson/S. Svedberg—Saab Sport
3 B. Waldegaard/L. Nystrom—VW 1500S

East African Safari
1 J. Singh/J. Singh—Volvo
2 I. Jaffray/S. Bathurst—Peugeot 404
3 V. Preston/E. Syder—Ford Cortina

Tulip Rally
Touring category
1 H. Lund/B. Wahlgren—Saab 96
2 O. Dahl/L. Haag—Saab 96
3 T. Makinen/P. Easter—Mini-Cooper 'S'

Grand Touring category
1 R. Smith/V. Domleo—Hillman Imp
2 I. Lewis/D. Pollard—Hillman Imp
3 J. Thuner/J. Gretener—Triumph 2000

Acropolis Rally
1 C. Skogh/L. Berggren—Volvo 122S
2 E. Carlsson/T. Ahman—Saab 96 Sport
3 R. Trautmann/C. Bouchet—Lancia Flavia

Geneva Rally
1 R. Aaltonen/A. Ambrose—Mini-Cooper 'S'
2 R. Trautmann/C. Bouchet—Lancia Flavia
3 S. Zasada/K. Osinski—Steyr-Puch 650T

Scottish Rally
1 R. Clark/J. Porter—Ford Cortina GT
2 I. Lewis/R. Turvey—Hillman Imp
3 L. Morrison/J. Syer—Rover 2000

Circuit of Ireland Rally
1 P. Hopkirk/T. Harryman—Mini-Cooper 'S'
2 V. Elford/D. Stone—Ford Cortina GT
3 R. Clark/J. Porter—Ford Cortina GT

Czech Rally
1 R. Aaltonen/A. Ambrose—Mini-Cooper 'S'
2 R. Trautmann/C. Bouchet—Lancia Flavia
3 G. Pianta/L. Lombardini—Lancia Flavia

Alpine Rally
1 R. Trautmann/C. Bouchet—Lancia Flavia
2 T. Makinen/P. Easter—Mini-Cooper 'S'
3 H. Taylor/B. Melia—Ford Lotus Cortina

Polish Rally
1 R. Aaltonen/A. Ambrose—Mini-Cooper 'S'
2 S. Zasada/K. Osinski—Steyr-Puch 650T
3 E. Carlsson/T. Ahman—Saab Sport

Finnish 1000 Lakes Rally
1 T. Makinen/P. Keskitalo—Mini-Cooper 'S'
2 R. Aaltonen/A. Jarvi—Mini-Cooper 'S'
3 P. Toivonen/K. Leivo—Volkswagen 1500S

Munich-Vienna-Budapest Rally
1 R. Aaltonen/A. Ambrose—Mini-Cooper 'S'
2 . Tunner/ . Hick—Ford Cortina GT
3 A. Pilhatsch/ . Lederer—BMW 1800TI

RAC Rally
1 R. Aaltonen/A. Ambrose—Mini-Cooper 'S'
2 T. Makinen/P. Easter—Austin-Healey 3000
3 J. Larsson/L. Lundblad—Saab Sport 96

1966

Monte Carlo Rally
1 P. Toivonen/E. Mikander—Citroen DS21
2 R. Trautmann/J. Hanrioud—Lancia Flavia
3 O. Andersson/R. Dahlgren—Lancia Flavia

Swedish Rally
1 A. Andersson/S. Svedberg—Saab Sport
2 S. Lampinen/B. Olsson—Saab Sport
3 T. Trana/S. Andreasson—Volvo 122S

Italian Rally of the Flowers
1 L. Cella/L. Lombardini—Lancia Fulvia
2 G. Klass/R. Buchet—Porsche 911
3 O. Andersson/R. Dahlgren—Lancia Fulvia

East African Safari
1 R. Shankland/C. Rothwell—Peugeot 404
2 V. Preston/R. Gerrish—Ford Cortina
3 J. Singh/B. Chardway—Volvo

Circuit of Ireland Rally
1 A. Fall/H. Liddon—Mini-Cooper 'S'
2 B. Melia/G. Davies—Ford Lotus Cortina
3 A. Boyd/B. Crawford—Ford Cortina GT

Tulip Rally
1 R. Aaltonen/H. Liddon—Mini-Cooper 'S'
2 V. Elford/J. Davenport—Ford Lotus Cortina
3 P. Harper/R. Turvey—Sunbeam Tiger

Austrian Alpine Rally
1 P. Hopkirk/R. Crellin—Mini-Cooper 'S'
2 G. Wallbrabenstein/ . Muller—Porsche 911
3 . Burkhardt/ . Koch-Bodes—
    Ford Taunus 20M

Acropolis Rally
1 B. Soderstrom/G. Palm—Ford Lotus Cortina
2 R. Clark/B. Melia—Ford Lotus Cortina
3 P. Hopkirk/R. Crellin—Mini-Cooper 'S'

Scottish Rally
1 A. Fall/M. Wood—Mini-Cooper 'S'
2 J. Larsson/L. Lundblad—Saab Sport
3 R. Smith/V. Domleo—Hillman Imp

Geneva Rally
1 G. Staepelaere/A. Aerts—
    Ford Lotus Cortina
2 A. Fall/H. Liddon—Mini-Cooper 'S'
3 J. Ogier/B. Ogier—Panhard 24CT

Czech Rally
1 R. Aaltonen/H. Liddon—Mini-Cooper 'S'
2 B. Soderstrom/G. Palm—Ford Lotus Cortina
3 T. Makinen/P. Easter—Mini-Cooper 'S'

German Rally
1 G. Klass/R. Wutherlich—Porsche 911
2 G. Cavallari/ . Salvay—Alfa Romeo GTA
3 O. Springer/ . —BMW 1800TI

Polish Rally
1 A. Fall/A. Krauklis—Mini-Cooper 'S'
2 T. Makinen/P. Easter—Mini-Cooper 'S'
3 S. Zasada/E. Zasada—Steyr-Puch

Finnish 1000 Lakes Rally
1 T. Makinen/P. Keskitalo—Mini-Cooper 'S'
2 T. Trana/S. Andreasson—Volvo 122S
3 R. Aaltonen/ . Nurminaa—Mini-Cooper 'S'

Alpine Rally
1 J. Rolland/G. Augias—Alfa Romeo GTA
2 R. Clark/B. Melia—Ford Lotus Cortina
3 R. Aaltonen/H. Liddon—Mini-Cooper 'S'

Munich-Vienna-Budapest Rally
1 T. Makinen/P. Easter—Mini-Cooper 'S'
2 L. Cella/L. Lombardini—Lancia Fulvia
3 L. Nasenius/F. Sager—Opel Rekord 1700

RAC Rally
1 B. Soderstrom/G. Palm—Ford Lotus Cortina
2 H. Kallstrom/R. Hakansson—
   Mini-Cooper 'S'
3 T. Trana/S. Andreasson—Volvo

1967

Monte Carlo Rally
1 R. Aaltonen/H. Liddon—Mini-Cooper 'S'
2 O. Andersson/J. Davenport—Lancia Fulvia
3 V. Elford/D. Stone—Porsche 911S

Swedish Rally
1 B. Soderstrom/G. Palm—Lotus Cortina
2 S. Lampinen/T. Palm—Saab V4
3 R. Aaltonen/H. Liddon—Mini-Cooper 'S'

Italian Rally of the Flowers
1 J. Piot/C. Roure—Renault Gordini R8
2 P. Hopkirk/R. Crellin—Mini-Cooper 'S'
3 O. Andersson/J. Davenport—Lancia Fulvia

Lyon-Charbonnieres Rally
1 V. Elford/D. Stone—Porsche 911S
2 J. Hanrioud/X. Foucher—Porsche 911S
3 S. Zasada/E. Pach—Porsche 911S

East African Safari
1 B. Shankland/C. Rothwell—Peugeot 404
2 V. Preston/R. Gerrish—Ford Lotus Cortina
3 P. Hughes/R. Syder—Ford Cortina GT

Circuit of Ireland
1 P. Hopkirk/T. Harryman—Mini-Cooper 'S'
2 A. Boyd/B. Crawford—Mini-Cooper 'S'
3 C. Gunn/N. Henderson—Ford Lotus Cortina

Tulip Rally
1 V. Elford/D. Stone—Porsche 911S
2 T. Makinen/P. Easter—Mini-Cooper 'S'
3 R. Aaltonen/H. Liddon—Mini-Cooper 'S'

Austrian Alpine Rally
1 S. Zasada/J. Dobranski—Porsche 911S
2 L. Jonsson/L. Eriksson—Saab V4
3 R. Bocknicek/G. Pfisterer—Citroen DS21

Acropolis Rally
1 P. Hopkirk/R. Crellin—Mini-Cooper 'S'
2 O. Andersson/J. Davenport—Lancia Fulvia
3 B. Soderstrom/G. Palm—Ford Lotus Cortina

Geneva Rally
1 V. Elford/D. Stone—Porsche 911S
2 S. Munari/G. Harris—Lancia Fulvia
3 A. Fall/M. Wood—Mini-Cooper 'S'

Czech Rally
1 E. Carlsson/T. Aman—Saab V4
2 S. Zasada/J. Dobranski—Porsche 912
3 P. Moss/E. Nystrom—Saab V4

Castrol-Danube Rally
1 A. Fall/M. Wood—Austin 1800
2 J. Vinatier/C. Roure—Renault Gordini R8
3 G. Wallbrabenstein/W. Bretthauer—Porsche

Polish Rally
1 S. Zasada/E. Zasada—Porsche 912
2 L. Nasenius/M. Wigren—Opel Rekord
3 K. Kormornicki/M. Wachowski—
   BMW 1600

Finnish 1000 Lakes Rally
1 T. Makinen/P. Keskitalo—Mini-Cooper 'S'
2 S. Lampinen/K. Sohlberg—Saab V4
3 H. Mikkola/A. Jarvi—Volvo 122S

Alpine Rally
1 P. Hopkirk/R. Crellin—Mini-Cooper 'S'
2 B. Consten/J. Peray—Alfa Romeo GTA
3 J. Gamet/M. Gamet—Alfa Romeo GTA

Scottish Rally
1 R. Clark/J. Porter—Ford Lotus Cortina
2 L. Ytterbring/L. Persson—Mini-Cooper 'S'
3 C. Orrenius/G. Schroderheim—Saab V4

Spanish Rally
1 O. Andersson/J. Davenport—Lancia Fulvia
2 S. Munari/L. Lombardini—Lancia Fulvia
3 B. Tramont/R. Munoz—Alpine-Renault

Munich-Vienna-Budapest Rally
1 J. Piot/J. Brenaud—Renault Gordini R8
2 B. Soderstrom/G. Palm—Ford Lotus Cortina
3 K. Reisch/H. Schwab—MG MGB

1968

Monte Carlo Rally
1 V. Elford/D. Stone—Porsche 911T
2 P. Toivonen/M. Tiukkanen—Porsche 911T
3 R. Aaltonen/H. Liddon—Mini-Cooper 'S'

Swedish Rally
1 B. Waldegaard/L. Helmer—Porsche 911T
2 T. Trana/S. Andreasson—Saab V4
3 H. Lindberg/B. Reinicke—Saab V4

Italian San Remo Rally
1 P. Toivonen/M. Tiukkanen—Porsche 911T
2 P. Moss/E. Nystrom—Lancia Fulvia
3 O. Andersson/J. Davenport—Ford Escort TC

East African Safari
1 N. Nowicki/P. Cliff—Peugeot 404
2 P. Huth/I. Grant—Ford Lotus Cortina
3 K. Mandeville/S. Allison—Triumph 2000

Circuit of Ireland
1 R. Clark/J. Porter—Ford Escort TC
2 A. Boyd/B. Crawford—Mini-Cooper 'S'
3 R. Smith/M. Lowrey—Sunbeam Imp

Tulip Rally
1 R. Clark/J. Porter—Ford Escort TC
2 O. Andersson/J. Davenport—Ford Escort TC
3 J. Vernaeve/M. Wood—Mini-Cooper 'S'

East German Rally
1 P. Toivonen/M. Kolari—Porsche 911T
2 S. Zasada/ . Porsche 911T
3 . Weiner/ . Karel—BMW

West German Rally
1 P. Toivonen/M. Kolari—Porsche 911T
2 S. Zasada/ . Postava—Porsche
3 J. Piot/ . Rousselot—Alpine-Renault

Austrian Alpine Rally
1 B. Soderstrom/G. Palm—Ford Escort TC
2 H. Mikkola/A. Jarvi—Lancia Fulvia
3 W. Roser/R. Loibnegger—
   Renault Gordini R8

Acropolis Rally
1 R. Clark/J. Porter—Ford Escort TC
2 S. Zasada/J. Dobranski—Porsche 911T
3 P. Toivonen/M. Kolari—Porsche 911T

Scottish Rally
1 R. Clark/J. Porter—Ford Escort TC
2 L. Ytterbring/L. Persson—Mini-Cooper 'S'
3 C. Malkin/J. Brown—Sunbeam Imp

Geneva Rally
1 P. Toivonen/ . Vihervaava—Porsche 911T
2 L. Bianchi/J. Jacquemin—Alfa Romeo GTA
3 G. Verrier/G. Murac—Alfa Romeo GTA

Czech Rally
1 J. Vinatier/M. Callewaert—Alpine-Renault
2 S. Lampinen/T. Palm—Saab V4
3 G. Staepelaere/A. Aerts—Ford Escort TC

Castrol-Danube Rally
1 P. Toivonen/M. Tiukkanen—Porsche 911T
2 W. Poltinger/ . Merinsky—Volvo 142S
3 . Dietmayer/ . Hahn—Lancia Fulvia

Finnish 1000 Lakes Rally
1 H. Mikkola/A. Jarvi—Ford Escort TC
2 S. Lampinen/K. Sohlberg—Saab V4
3 B. Soderstrom/G. Palm—Ford Escort TC

Alpine Rally
1 J. Vinatier/J. Jacob—Alpine-Renault
2 J. Barailler/J. Fayel—Alfa Romeo GTA
3 R. Trautmann/C. Trautmann—Lancia Fulvia

RAC Rally
1 S. Lampinen/J. Davenport—Saab V4
2 C. Orrenius/G. Schroderheim—Saab V4
3 J. Bullough/D. Barrow—Ford Escort TC

London-to-Sydney Marathon
1 A. Cowan/C. Malkin/B. Coyle—
   Hillman Hunter
2 P. Hopkirk/A. Nash/A. Poole—
   Austin 1800
3 I. Vaughan/R. Forsyth/J. Ellis—
   Ford Falcon GT

1969

Monte Carlo Rally
1 B. Waldegaard/L. Helmer—Porsche 911
2 G. Larrousse/J. Perramond—Porsche 911
3 J. Vinatier/J. Jacob—Alpine-Renault

Swedish Rally
1 B. Waldegaard/L. Helmer—Porsche 911
2 S. Lampinen/A. Hertz—Saab V4
3 O. Eriksson/H. Johansson—
   Opel Rallye Kadett

Italian Flowers Rally
1 H. Kallstrom/G. Haggbom—Lancia Fulvia
2 R. Aaltonen/H. Liddon—Lancia Fulvia
3 S. Barbasio/M. Mannucci—Lancia Fulvia

East African Safari
1 R. Hillyar/J. Aird—Ford Taunus
2 J. Singh/B. Bhardwaj—Volvo 142
3 J. Din/M. Minas—Datsun P510

Circuit of Ireland
1 R. Clark/J. Porter—Ford Escort TC
2 P. Hopkirk/A. Nash—Mini-Cooper 'S'
3 A. Boyd/B. Crawford—Mini-Cooper 'S'

Tulip Rally
1 G. Staepelaere/A. Aertz—Ford Escort TC
2 R. Slotemaker/F. van der Geest—
   BMW 2002TI
3 M. Lansjo/M. Sundin—Opel Rallye Kadett

Austrian Alpine Rally
1 H. Mikkola/M. Wood—Ford Escort TC
2 H. Kallstrom/G. Haggbom—Lancia Fulvia
3 S. Lampinen/A. Hertz—Saab V4

Acropolis Rally
1 P. Toivonen/M. Kolari—Porsche 911S
2 R. Clark/J. Porter—Ford Escort TC
3 C. Laurent/J. Marche—Daf 55

Scottish Rally
1 S. Lampinen/A. Hertz—Saab V4
2 A. Cowan/B. Coyle—Hillman Imp
3 M. Hibbert/I. Withers—Ford Escort TC

Czech Rally
1 G. Staepelaere/A. Aertz—Ford Escort TC
2 H. Kallstrom/G. Haggbom—Lancia Fulvia
3 . Hubacek/ . Reger—Renault Gordini

Polish Rally
1 S. Zasada/E. Zasada—Porsche 911S
2 G. Staepelaere/A. Aertz—Ford Escort TC
3 H. Kallstrom/G. Haggbom—Lancia Fulvia

Finnish 1000 Lakes Rally
1 H. Mikkola/A. Jarvi—Ford Escort TC
2 S. Lampinen/K. Sohlberg—Saab V4
3 R. Virtapuro/M. Tiukkanen—
   Opel Rallye Kadett

Alpine Rally
1 J. Vinatier/J. Jacob—Alpine-Renault
2 J. Andruet/P. Ecot—Alpine-Renault
3 J. Lusenius/S. Halme—Alpine-Renault

Three Cities Rally
1 W. Roser/L. Mayer—Alpine-Renault
2 J. Vinatier/C. Roure—Alpine-Renault
3 W. Poltinger/J. Hartinger—Porsche 911T

Spanish Rally
1 H. Kallstrom/G. Haggbom—Lancia Fulvia
2 G. Staepelaere/A. Aerts—Ford Escort TC
3 R. Pinto/A. Bernacchini—Lancia Fulvia

RAC Rally
1 H. Kallstrom/G. Haggbom—Lancia Fulvia
2 C. Orrenius/D. Stone—Saab V4
3 A. Fall/H. Liddon—Lancia Fulvia

1970

Monte Carlo Rally
1 B. Waldegaard/L. Helmer—Porsche 911S
2 G. Larrousse/M. Gelin—Porsche 911S
3 J. Nicolas/C. Roure—Alpine-Renault

Swedish Rally
1 B. Waldegaard/L. Helmer—Porsche 911S
2 S. Blomqvist/B. Reinicke—Saab V4
3 L. Nasenius/B. Cederberg—
   Opel Rallye Kadett

San Remo-Sestriere Rally
1 J. Therier/M. Callewaert—Alpine-Renault
2 H. Kallstrom/G. Haggbom—Lancia Fulvia
3 J. Vinatier/J. Jacob—Alpine-Renault

East African Safari
1 E. Herrmann/H. Schuller—Datsun 1600SSS
2 J. Singh/K. Ranyard—Datsun 1600SSS
3 B. Shankland/C. Rothwell—Peugeot 504

Circuit of Ireland
1 R. Clark/J. Porter—Ford Escort TC
2 C. Sclater/P. Valentine—Ford Escort TC
3 J. Henriksson/L. Carlstrom—
   Opel Rallye Kadett

Austrian Alpine Rally
1 B. Waldegaard/L. Nystrom—Porsche 911S
2 H. Lindberg/S. Andreasson—Saab 96
3 J. Piot/J. Todt—Ford Escort TC

Scottish Rally
1 B. Culcheth/J. Syer—Triumph 2.5PI
2 P. Hopkirk/A. Nash—Mini Clubman 1275
3 R. McBurney/N. Smith—BMW 2002TI

Acropolis Rally
1 J. Therier/M. Callewaert—Alpine-Renault
2 J. Vinatier/D. Stone—Alpine-Renault
3 O. Andersson/J. Porter—Ford Escort TC

Finnish 1000 Lakes Rally
1 H. Mikkola/G. Palm—Ford Escort TC
2 T. Makinen/H. Liddon—Ford Escort TC
3 S. Lampinen/J. Davenport—Lancia Fulvia

RAC Rally
1 H. Kallstrom/G. Haggbom—Lancia Fulvia
2 O. Eriksson/H. Johansson—
   Opel Rallye Kadett
3 L. Nasenius/B. Cederberg—
   Opel Rallye Kadett

Tulip Rally
1 C. van Grieken/M. Verbunt—BMW 2002TI
2 J. Ragnotti/P. Thimonier—Opel Rallye Kadett
3 S. Barbasio/M. Mannucci—Lancia Fulvia

Geneva Rally
1 J. Andruet/M. Veron—Alpine-Renault
2 J. Nicolas/J. Todt—Alpine-Renault
3 J. Maurin/J. Maurier—Alpine-Renault

Moldau Rally
1 G. Staepelaere/A. Aerts—Ford Escort TC
2 H. Kallstrom/G. Haggbom—Lancia Fulvia
3 W. Roser/R. Loibnegger—Alpine-Renault

Polish Rally
1 J. Andruet/M. Veron—Alpine-Renault
2 S. Zasada/E. Zasada—Porsche 911S
3 G. Staepelaere/A. Aerts—Ford Escort TC

Castrol-Danube Rally
1 G. Janger/W. Wessiak—Porsche 911S
2 C. Schindler/G. Hruschka—Porsche 914/6
3 N. Hollier/P. Short—Alpine-Renault

Three Cities Rally
1 J. Andruet/M. Veron—Alpine-Renault
2 J. Nicolas/M. Callewaert—Alpine-Renault
3 G. Staepelaere/A. Aerts—Ford Escort TC

Portuguese TAP Rally
1 S. Lampinen/J. Davenport—Lancia Fulvia
2 S. Munari/A. Bernacchini—Lancia Fulvia
3 B. Waldegaard/B. Thorszelius—Porsche 911

London-to-Mexico World Cup Rally
1 H. Mikkola/G. Palm—Ford Escort TC
2 B. Culcheth/J. Syer—Triumph 2.5PI
3 R. Aaltonen/H. Liddon—Ford Escort TC

Monte Carlo Rally
1 O. Andersson/D. Stone—Alpine-Renault
2 J. Therier/M. Callewaert—Alpine-Renault
3 = J. Andruet/G. Vial—Alpine-Renault
    B. Waldegaard/H. Thorszelius—Porsche 914/6

Swedish Rally
1 S. Blomqvist/A. Hertz—Saab V4
2 L. Nystrom/G. Nystrom—BMW 2002TI
3 H. Kallstrom/G. Haggbom—Lancia Fulvia

San Remo Sestriere Rally
1 O. Andersson/A. Nash—Alpine-Renault
2 A. Ballestriere/A. Bernacchini—Lancia Fulvia
3 S. Barbasio/P. Sodano—Lancia Fulvia

East African Safari
1 E. Herrmann/H. Schuller—Datsun 240Z
2 S. Mehta/M. Doughty—Datsun 240Z
3 B. Shankland/C. Bates—Peugeot 504

Circuit of Ireland
1 A. Boyd/B. Crawford—Ford Escort TC
2 C. Sclater/M. Holmes—Ford Escort RS1600
3 W. Coleman/D. O'Sullivan—Ford Escort TC

Morocco Rally
1 J. Deschazeaux/J. Plassard—Citroen SM
2 G. Chasseuil/C. Baron—Peugeot 504
3 B. Consten/S. Motte—Citroen DS21

Austrian Alpine Rally
1 O. Andersson/A. Hertz—Alpine-Renault 1600
2 A. Paganelli/D. Russo—Fiat 124 Spyder
3 K. Russling/F. Mikes—VW 1302 S

Acropolis Rally
1 O. Andersson/A. Hertz—Alpine-Renault 1600
2 J. Nicolas/G. Vial—Alpine-Renault 1600
3 S. Lampinen/J. Davenport—Lancia Fulvia

Scottish Rally
1 C. Sclater/J. Davenport—Ford Escort RS1600
2 M. Hibbert/H. Scott—Ford Escort TC
3 R. Fidler/B. Hughes—Ford Escort RS 1600

Alpine Rally
1 B. Darniche/J. Mahe—Alpine-Renault 1600
2 J. Vinatier/L. Pointet—Alpine-Renault 1600
3 J. Piot/J. Porter—Ford Escort RS 1600

RAC Rally
1 S. Blomqvist/A. Hertz—Saab 96 V4
2 B. Waldegaard/L. Nystrom—Porsche 911S
3 C. Orrenius/L. Persson—Saab 96 V4

European Rally Champions
1960	W. Schock—Mercedes
1961	H. J. Walter—Porsche
1962	E. Bohringer—Mercedes
1963	G. Andersson—Volvo
1964	T. Trana—Volvo
1965	R. Aaltonen—Mini-Cooper
1966	L. Nasenius (Group 1)—Opel
	S. Zasada (Group 2)—Porsche
	G. Klass (Group 3)—Porsche
1967	S. Zasada (Group 1)—Porsche
	B. Soderstrom (Group 2)—Ford
	V. Elford (Group 3)—Porsche
1968	P. Toivonen—Porsche
1969	H. Kallstrom—Lancia
1970	J. C. Andruet—Alpine-Renault
1971	S. Zasada—BMW

European Rally Championship for Manufacturers
1968	Ford (GB)
1969	Ford (Europe)
1970	Porsche
1971	Alpine-Renault

RAC Rally Champions
1960	W. Bengry
1961	W. Bengry
1962	A. Fisher
1963	A. Fisher
1964	E. Jackson
1965	R. Clark
1966	R. Fidler
1967	J. Bullough
1968	C. Malkin
1969	J. Bloxham
1970	W. Sparrow
1971	C. Sclater

Motoring News Rally Championship
	Drivers	Navigators
1961	W. Bengry	B. Melia
1962	A. Fisher	B. Melia
1963	R. McBride	D. Barrow
1964	R. McBride	D. Barrow
1965	G. Bloom	A. Taylor
1966	M. Gibbs	R. Morgan
1967	J. Bullough	D. Barrow
1968	C. Malkin	J. Brown
1969	J. Bloxham	R. Harper
1970	J. Bullough	D. Barrow
1971	G. Hill	K. Wood

Car manufacturers' addresses

ALPINE-RENAULT
Société des Automobile Alpine,
13 Rue Forest,
Paris, France
(Seine 55B-9487)
J. Cheinisse

BLMC
British Leyland Motor Corporation Ltd,
Special Tuning Department,
Abingdon, Berkshire
(Abingdon 251)
B. Wales

BMW
BMW AG,
Lerchenauerstr 76,
D.8000,
Munchen 13,
Germany
(0811-38951)

BMW
BMW-Steinmetz,
Steinmetz-Automobiltechnik,
Pommernstrasse, 8
D.609
Russelsheim,
Germany
(06142-52045)

CHRYSLER
Chrysler UK,
PO Box 25,
Competitions Department,
Humber Road,
Coventry CV3 1BD
(52144)
D. O'Dell

CITROEN
Citroen SA,
Quai André Citroen 133,
Paris 13, France
Madame Coton

DAF
Van Doorne's Automobielfabrieken NV,
Geldropseweg 303,
Eindhoven,
Holland
R. Koch

DATSUN
Nissan Motor Co Ltd,
17-1, 6 Chome Ginza,
Chuo-Ku, Tokyo
(03.543.5523)
R. Nakagawa

FIAT
Fiat SA,
Direzione Assistenza Technica Automobilistica,
Via Bethollet 46,
10125 Torino,
Italy

FORD (UK)
Ford Motor Co Ltd,
Competitions Department,
Boreham Airfield,
Chelmsford,
Essex
(Boreham 661)
S. Turner

FORD (GERMANY)
Ford Werke AG,
Motorsportabteilung,
Henry Ford Strasse,
D.5000,
Koln-Niehl,
Germany
(0221.7103380)
J. Neerpasch

LANCIA
HF Squadra Corse Lancia,
Via V. Lancia 27,
10141 Torino,
Italy
(3331)
C. Fiorio

PORSCHE
Dr Ing F. Porsche KG,
Porschestrasse 42,
D.7000,
Stuttgart-Zuffenhausen,
Germany
(0711.82031)

SAAB
Saab-Scania,
461-01 Trollhattan,
Sweden
(0520-12600)
B. Hellberg

VOLVO
Volvo AB,
S.405.08,
Goteborg, Sweden
G. Andersson

APPENDIX 5
Useful trade addresses

JOHN ALEY RACING LTD,
63 Ditton Walk,
Cambridge
(Teversham 3293, Sawston 2356)

ARMSTRONG PATENTS CO LTD,
Beverley,
Yorkshire
(Beverley 882212)
L. Banks

AUTOLITE MOTOR PRODUCTS LTD,
Wharf Road,
Ponders End,
Enfield, Middlesex
(01-804 1221)
B. Melia

AUTOMOTIVE PRODUCTS CO LTD,
Tachbrook Road,
Leamington Spa,
Warwickshire
(Leamington Spa 27000)
J. Moore

BILSTEIN, AUGUST
D.5828, Ennepetal-Altenvoerde,
Hugo Emde,
Germany
(02333-65351)

BOSCH, ROBERT
D.7141, Schwieberdingen,
Fritz Juttner,
Germany
(0711–8118245)

BRITAX LTD
Proctor Works,
Chertsey Road,
Byfleet, Surrey
(Byfleet 41121)
P. Darley

CASTROL UK
Burmah-Castrol House,
Marylebone Road,
London NW1 5AA
(01-486 4455)
R. Willis

CASTROL GERMANY
Schaferkampsalle 18,
Hamburg 6
(41141)

CASTROL ITALY
Via Aosta 4a,
Casella Postale 3343,
Milano
(Milano 313341)

CHAMPION SPARKING PLUG CO LTD
Feltham,
Middlesex
(01-759 6442)
L. Hands

DUNLOP UK
Fort Dunlop,
Erdington,
Birmingham 24
(021-373 2121)
J. Ferguson

DUNLOP GERMANY
Dunlop AG,
Postfach 129,
D.645 Hanau
(06181.861624)
G. Weber

ELF
12 Rue Jean Nicot,
75 Paris 7,
France
M. Dehaye

FERODO LTD
Chapel-en-le-Frith,
Stockport, Cheshire
(Chapel 2520)
A. Campbell

GIRLING LTD
Kings Road,
Tyseley,
Birmingham 11
(021-706 3371)
J. F. Wood

GOODYEAR TYRE AND RUBBER CO LTD
Wolverhampton, Staffs
(Wolverhampton 22321)
S. Moggridge

KONI NV
POB 14,
Oud Beyerland,
Holland
(01860.2500)

KONI UK
J. W. E. Banks & Sons,
Crowland,
Peterborough PE6 0JP
(Crowland 316)
G. B. Holland

JOSEPH LUCAS LTD
Great King Street,
Birmingham 19
(021-554 5252)
R. Wood

126

MICHELIN
97 Boulevard Pereire,
75 Paris 17,
France
A. Chevalier

MINILITE
Tech Del Ltd,
32-36 Telford Way,
Acton,
London W3
(01-743 0103)

SHELL
Shell Centre,
Waterloo,
London SE1
(01-934 6525)
K. Ballisat

SMITHS INDUSTRIES LTD
Motor Accessory Division,
50 Oxgate Lane,
Cricklewood,
London NW2
(01-452 3333)
J. Owens

APPENDIX 6

Organisers of major international rallies

ACROPOLIS RALLY
Automobile Touring Club of Greece,
6 Rue Amerikis,
Athens 134,
Greece
(638.520)

ALPINE RALLY
ASAC Marseille & Provence,
27 Cours Pierre Puget,
13 Marseille,
France
(37.33.61)

AUSTRIAN ALPINE RALLY
OAMTC,
Schubertring 3,
A-1010 Wien,
Austria
(0222.927651)

CIRCUIT OF IRELAND
Ulster Automobile Club,
3 Botanic Avenue,
Belfast BT7 1JG
Northern Ireland
(21607)

EAST AFRICAN SAFARI
Automobile Association of East Africa,
PO Box 87,
Nairobi,
Kenya
(28317)

MONTE CARLO RALLY
Automobile Club de Monaco,
23 Boulevard Albert 1er,
Monaco
(30.32.20)

MOROCCO RALLY
Association Sportive du Royal Automobile
Club Morocain,
4 Rue Chappe,
BP 598,
Casablanca
Morocco
(632.66)

POLISH RALLY
Automobilklub Krakowski,
Krakow
Poland
(Solskiego 33)

RAC RALLY
Royal Automobile Club,
31 Belgrave Square,
London SW1
(01-235 8601)

RALLYE VLTAVA
UAMK CSSR,
Opletalova 29,
Praha
Czechoslovakia

SAN REMO-SESTRIERE RALLY
Automobile Club Torino,
Via Giolitti 15,
10123 Torino
Italy
(5779)

SCOTTISH RALLY
Royal Scottish Automobile Club,
11 Blythswood Square,
Glasgow C2
(041-221 3850)

SPANISH RALLY
Real Automovil Club de Espana,
General Sanjurjo 10,
Madrid 3
Spain
(257.60.05)

SWEDISH RALLY
KAK,
103.20 Stockholm 16
Sweden
(23.88.00)

TAP RALLY
Grupo Cultural e Desportivo da TAP,
Aeroporto da Portela,
Lisbon,
Portugal

1000 LAKES RALLY
Suomen Autoklubi,
Hotelli Rantasipi,
Jyväskyla,
Finland
(22122)

TOUR DE CORSE
ASAC de la Corse Essitac,
Hotel de Ville,
20, Ajaccio,
Corsica
(14.07)

TOUR DE FRANCE
ASA du Tour de France
136 Rue de Longchamp,
75 Paris 16,
France

TULIP RALLY
Stichting Internationale Tulpen Rallye Holland,
Hoogstraat 119,
Schiedam,
Holland
(010.263537)